JUST A MINUTE

TEN SHORT PLAYS AND ACTIVITIES FOR YOUR CLASSROOM

With rehearsal strategies
to accompany multicultural
stories from around the world

Irene N. Watts

Pembroke Publishers Limited

For Adam and Matthew

Pembroke Publishers Limited
528 Hood Road
Markham, Ontario
L3R 3K9

Canadian Cataloguing in Publication Data

Watts, Irene N., 1931-
  Just a minute: ten short plays and activities
for your classroom

ISBN 0-921217-53-6

1. Drama - Study and teaching (Elementary).
2. Children's plays, Canadian (English).*
I. Title.

PN3171.W37 1990   372.6′6′044   C90-095073-0

Published in the U.S.A. by
Heinemann Educational Books, Inc.
361 Hanover St.
Portsmouth, N.H. 03801

Editor: David Kilgour
Design: Falcom Design

Printed and bound in Canada
9 8 7 6 5 4 3 2 1

Contents

Foreword

I have never quite known how to repay the enormous debt I owe Irene Watts.

In the early 1970's when I was asked to take over the direction of **The Citadel Theatre** in Edmonton, Alberta, I was fortunate in that an important plank of that theatre's work was a small group of actors, separate from the main company, that toured the schools of Alberta with special programs directed at young audiences. The *Citadel-On-Wheels* was very dear to my heart. In truth it was the main reason I joined **The Citadel**, having founded a similar program in England. I was even more fortunate that Irene Watts was the director of this project. From her I learned a great deal about this vitally important work. We enjoyed a warm and fruitful collaboration over a number of years.

Some six years later I became the Director of the **Neptune Theatre** in Halifax, Nova Scotia. They had no such program and the theatre was heavily in debt. However, I was determined that Neptune should undertake this responsibility. We had no money. I called Irene. She flew from Vancouver, started up *Young Neptune* (at ridiculously miniscule wages) and directed the first season in which we serviced well over one hundred schools. Again I learned much about Irene's dedication to young audiences.

She is quite simply the best in her field on this continent, perhaps in the English-speaking world.

On reading this volume I am confident you will agree.

JOHN NEVILLE

About This Book

Just a Minute is intended to bridge the gap between improvised drama and the scripted play. Students differ widely in their readiness for scripted work, but the material in this book is aimed primarily at ages ten to fifteen. Continued improvisatory and exploratory work as part of the rehearsal process is emphasized in each of the drama activities for each play, which suggest exercises for mime, movement, characterization, language, and narrative voice work. Although each activity unit relates specifically to the play it follows, several can be adapted for use with more than one play.

There is sufficient material in each section to cover many rehearsal/drama periods. Teachers need not follow the ideas consecutively, but can select one or two as appropriate to meet the needs of the group.

All the plays are based on folktales and legends, and have been chosen as examples of particular cultures. Characters are broadly drawn and plots involve powerful, universal themes that students can identify with: life and death; the natural and supernatural; greed and generosity; honesty and deceit.

The theme of multiculturalism is present in both the plays and the accompanying activities. (The next chapter will identify some further strategies that have universal application.) The plays are not graded in difficulty, but present different kinds of challenges to the students: *The Enchanted Spring*, for example, is a thinly disguised allegory about the discrimination faced by minority groups. *The Pied Piper of Hamelin* is a verse play with speaking parts for a cast of twenty-seven. *Earth, Fire, and Water* makes demands in mime and movement, as does *The Captive Moon*.

The plays are very short, ranging in length from three or four to ten or twelve minutes. They are designed to work in any space and with very simple staging. Some suggestions are given for presentation, but students will benefit from their own creative input. For those occasions when a longer and more formal presentation is required, a combination of a number of the plays involving a linking theme — greed, compassion, the supernatural, etc. — or emphasizing a contrast of plot would work well. For example, the significance of light and darkness, and their influence on people's behavior, could be explored in both *Sungold* and *The Captive Moon*, or the theme of breaking one's word in *The Pied Piper of Hamelin* and *Good Neighbors*. And the power of water runs through *Earth, Fire, and Water, The Talking Fish, The Enchanted Spring,* and *The Magic Sieve.*

Programs could vary in length ranging from twenty minutes to an hour. The key is flexibility in casting, staging, and programming.

Acknowledgments

I am grateful for the generous and creative ideas of the many students I have worked with over the years. Also, I would like to acknowledge the financial support of the Secretary of State, Multiculturalism Canada in helping me to complete this book.

Drama and Multiculturalism in the Classroom

*I*n North America today, many different languages, customs, and cultures jostle for our attention. Drama can help students recognize and accept these differences. Good theatre deals with such universal human truths as love, fear, hatred, hope, and the struggle for survival. Drama can become a unifying factor, celebrating both our differences and those things we share, thereby enriching us as human beings and as artists.

The activities that follow each play in this book contain discussion points and exercises that are relevant to drama in the multicultural classroom. The following ideas, ranging from simple physical exercises to more complex class discussions, are intended to be used in a more general way; they are applicable to all the plays and may also be adapted to stand alone.

1. Breathing circle

Students stand in well spaced groups of five or six, in a circle facing inward. The exercise begins with a quiet moment when each student becomes aware of the rhythm of his or her own breathing. The teacher quietly explains that each time they exhale, the students should allow their bodies to sag with the breath, so that gradually each breath brings them lower until they reach the floor. Students relax completely for about ten seconds before slowly coming to a sitting position. They all work at their own pace; there is no right or wrong way to do this. The group should remain silent until all the students in each group are sitting again.

This is an excellent beginning or ending to a class, as it releases tension and helps students to concentrate.

2. Portraits

Students are reminded that each character in a play or story has a life history, which the actor portrays, and that each person moves in a unique way. The class is asked to sit in a circle on the floor, and then the students introduce themselves as though introducing new characters: the idea is to build up portraits of "Who I am". Students give their names, favorite foods, hobbies, likes and dislikes, and share something of their family backgrounds.

Students (working individually but simultaneously in their own spaces) are asked to express this information as part of their own personal movement pattern. This may be quite short — e.g., Raika expresses in movement that she is shy but loves to dance; Andrew enacts his dislike of conformity through movement.

This work may later be shared by groups, or by the whole class. When possible, it should be done in a gym or any other large open space.

3. Similarities and contrasts

What kinds of things do people have in common? In the plays in this book many of the characters share certain traits — e.g., the family Li in *Earth, Fire, and Water* and the people of Hamelin in *The Pied Piper* appear to be at the mercy of their rulers. Dissatisfaction and greed are important elements in *The Talking Fish* and *The Magic Sieve*. Groups of five or six are asked to brainstorm their ideas and then to collectively write out their findings. Groups compare their thoughts, which are listed on the board under the heading "THINGS IN COMMON".

The exercise can also be repeated, this time listing differences. It will be apparent to the students that similarities outweigh differences.

4. Attitudes and changes

Using a similar technique, the class identifies attitudes 100 years ago to, for example, the role of women in society, children in the workforce, an acceptance of or discrimination against other cultures.

5. Quests and journeys

In stories and plays through the ages, the central character often goes on a journey to find the answer to a problem; in doing so he or she must first overcome physical or spiritual obstacles — e.g., the boy Israel in *The Enchanted Spring* seeks to destroy a curse put on his people; the daughter in *Sungold* cannot find happiness until she is honest about her roots. With encouragement from the teacher, students may be able to identify similar journeys in TV shows and movies they watch. They can share the kind of journeys and obstacles each one of them would have to face in overcoming a problem.

6. New beginnings

In this activity, the teacher encourages student discussion on reasons for leaving one's home or country: what are the reasons for making such a decision? Do emigrants have regrets, or does their success in a new country usually outweigh these? What kinds of contributions might they make to their new home?

The discussion begins with reasons for leaving home mentioned in the plays — e.g., the father in *Earth, Fire, and Water* is forced to leave his home to fight for a foreign cause, and dies far from his family. In small groups of five to eight, more personal examples and ideas drawn from the students' own experience may be used as topics for further discussion and dramatic exploration.

7. Teaching a new language

An idea common to many folk stories is that a human being is able to understand the language of living things — e.g., the boy understands the language of the loons in *The Blind Hunter*, and Israel understands the birds in *The Enchanted Spring*.

Ask students to imagine they have the ability to master any kind of language. Then, in pairs or threes, students may take turns to teach each other some words from a real or imaginary language.

This exercise works on several levels, in that it makes students aware of how difficult it is to speak an unfamiliar language, and offers ESL students the opportunity to teach.

8. Special objects

The Pied Piper has an enchanted flute, Israel a special jug, the wife receives a sieve with an inexhaustible supply of food, the wise woman has a mirror that reflects past events.

Ask students to bring any treasured object from home. Each day, ask, "Which objects shall we work with today?" The class then selects one or two and creates an original story about the object. The story may be stimulated by the teacher asking simple questions such as: "Where was this found?" "Who used to own this?" "What kind of special properties does it possess?"

After the story is completed (the exercise may be done in smaller groups and then shared with the class), the student who brought the object contributes his or her own reasons or those of the family for valuing the object.

9. Tribal skills and cultural contributions

Working as partners, pairs of students are told to imagine that "You are a member of an ancient tribe, and it is important that you pass on certain tribal skills to us — a game, a custom, a new form of writing, or a philosophy."

Pairs exchange skills, then form groups and decide *as groups* to teach the class a song, a custom, a story, or a skill from any of the groups' own ethnic backgrounds.

10. Emotions

Drama is about how people react under different circumstances, usually at a moment of crisis. For example, in *Sungold*, the daughter is accused of deceiving her mother because of greed. In *The Magic Sieve*, the brother is refused help by his rich sister and must break the shameful news to his wife. In *Good Neighbors*, a merchant is on the point of bankruptcy because of her neighbor's sharp business practices. In portraying these kinds of characters and their conflicting emotions, actors must use their imaginations and their own experiences of a variety of feelings to make the dramatic situation believable to an audience.

Students start off by thinking about incidents in their own lives which made them laugh or cry, feel love, anger, or fear. They are asked to recall individually specific information about the circumstances — e.g., where they were, the time of day when it happened, who else was there, even what the weather was like at the time. These remembered details will make the emotion felt more clear. Students then share some of their memories, which become the basis for further discussion and dramatization. A simple example would be the happiness felt on coming home from school on a sunny day, and finding a parcel with a surprise present from a dear friend.

Fear is one of the emotions most frequently expressed by children. In the plays in this book, characters are afraid of poverty (*Good Neighbors*), humiliation (*The Party, The Magic Sieve*, and *Sungold*), the supernatural and wild animals (*The Pied Piper of Hamelin*), and starvation and oppression (*Earth, Fire, and Water*), just to name a few fears.

Ask students to draw or write about as many of their own fears, or those of characters in the plays, as they wish. Small groups then share ideas and compare similarities and differences. Finally they present the different fears in the form of a human sculpture or film still — that is, they freeze the moment of fear in a tableau.

11. Celebration

Many special events are celebrated in the plays. The moon returns to the sky and the long darkness ends in *The Captive Moon*. In *The Magic Sieve* the brother and his wife invite the whole neighborhood to a New Year's party. In *The Party*, the village girls have a costume party just to celebrate the weekend.

After a class discussion of the kinds of celebrations that happen in different countries and ethnic communities, groups of students may dramatize a celebration based either on one of the events in the plays or on one of their own choice.

12. Minorities

"I get real mad when someone calls me a Chink."

"I feel the whole world's against me."

"When I was younger I used to wish I was white, they used to call me burnt toast and I really wished I was white. I found out you can let yourself be open and be what you are. I'm a Hindu and proud of it. Some people change their whole self to fit in with the crowd. I pity them."

"Being called a name, it's like nails on a chalkboard, running up and down my spine."

"Two Grade 6 boys put a note on my desk that said 'Kill the Jews'."

"I wish everybody could look into a person rather than just look at them and judge. If people could see what other people were really like from the inside, that would be an ideal kind of world."*

In this collection of plays, *The Enchanted Spring* concerns a witch (a thinly disguised reference to the authorities of the time) who dislikes Jews and therefore does everything in her power to hurt them. This play is based on an Eastern European story of the 18th century. Students need to be aware that racism and name calling are not confined to any one country or era.

In this exercise the class is asked to dramatize scenes of racism out of their own experiences and to come up with possible solutions for such offences. These scenes may be performed in any size of grouping, then discussed by the class for realism of content and character, and approach to overcoming the problem.

These are just some of the activities you can use with the plays in this book. Further multicultural activities, dealing specifically with the plays, are to be found in the activities listed after each play. And, of course, you may want to add your own.

---

* Student quotes include those from a dance/theatre piece, *Behind the Mask*. Original interviews conducted by Peg Campbell. Scripted by Irene N. Watts.

Good Neighbors

Cast

RICH MERCHANT *Male / Female*
POOR MERCHANT *Male / Female*
RICH MERCHANT'S CHILD *Male / Female*
NARRATOR *Male / Female*
CUSTOMERS *Any number, as required*

Staging

As with the other plays in this collection, this one works well in any kind of space. The group may decide that the entire set and props can be mimed, which would present one kind of challenge, and perhaps tie in with all kinds of occupational mime activities worked on in previous drama classes. Alternatively, if working within a basic set, two tables or desks at a short distance from each other with six-foot-long planks laid across their tops make good store fronts. A small folding screen behind each "store" also facilitates entrances and exits.

Props

Cookware, such as pots and pans, cutlery, kettles, etc.
Shopping bags for customers.
A ball.
Two reversible signs reading "OPEN" and "CLOSED" for the store fronts.

Costumes

Contemporary, requiring only an apron and cap for each of the merchants. Or they may be appropriate to any country that students wish to feature.

The play is written for females, but with minor changes of dialogue may be played by males. For example, father and son may be substituted for mother and daughter.

Good Neighbors

Adapted from "The Two Merchants"
by L. Tolstoy

NARRATOR: This story is about buying and selling, and it takes place in a market. It happened a long time ago, but it could happen today.
Once upon a time there were two merchants.

Two counters are set up by the merchants side by side, facing the audience.

RICH MERCHANT: One was successful.

POOR MERCHANT: The other was not.

Both try to attract customers, the rich merchant always going one better.

POOR MERCHANT: Best-quality kettles, only $3.00 each.

RICH MERCHANT: Kettles guaranteed to last a lifetime, $2.50 each. Buy here!

POOR MERCHANT: I've got saucepans made right here in town, excellent workmanship.

RICH MERCHANT: We're overstocked in cookware, we sell the same product cheaper.

Customers who are at the poor merchant's counter gradually move over to the rich merchant's counter and spend their money there.

POOR MERCHANT: The poor merchant decided that perhaps she should take a trip around the province and see how business was done elsewhere. She decided to ask her friend to take care of her stock while she was away.

She brings over all her goods. The rich merchant's daughter plays nearby.

RICH MERCHANT: Of course, I'll take care of your merchandise, just as though it were my own. Don't worry about anything. Have a good trip.

Poor merchant begins her journey. Exit.

RICH MERCHANT: She'll never be back, she said to her child. Off you go and play.

(*calling loudly*) Liquidation sale, don't miss it. Bankrupt stock, rock-bottom prices!

Customers congregate and buy up goods.

And the rich merchant sold all the poor merchant's stock that she was supposed to take care of, and made a very good profit.

POOR MERCHANT: After some months away, the poor merchant came home and went to the rich merchant to get back her stock.

RICH MERCHANT: (*aside*) I'm going to have to get out of this one fast. (*to poor merchant*) I'm so glad to see you, dear, but I'm afraid I have some bad news for you.

CHILD: Do you know what happened? Mum sold. . .

RICH MERCHANT: (*to child*) Go and play with your new ball, we're busy right now. (*to poor merchant*) I put all your stock in my shed over the winter, and the mice must have got at it. It was so damaged I just had to get rid of everything. I'm very sorry, but you do understand, don't you?

POOR MERCHANT: Oh, yes, I understand quite well. After all, I've seen many strange things on my travels. Goodbye. (*aside*) I know I've been deceived.

Rich merchant remains behind counter.

CHILD: The rich merchant's child was playing and wanted to hear all about the poor merchant's trip.

POOR MERCHANT: So the poor merchant and the child sat and talked for a while.

Improvised dialogue.

RICH MERCHANT: The rich merchant called her child for supper. Jenny!

POOR MERCHANT: The poor merchant decided she would teach her neighbor a lesson. She had never believed her story of the mice for a moment.

The poor merchant tells the child to hide, as a surprise.

RICH MERCHANT: The neighbor was getting worried. (*to poor merchant*) That child is never late for supper. Have you seen her anywhere?

POOR MERCHANT: Oh, yes, I have. A huge eagle swooped her up in his claws and they went flying out over the bay, just a moment ago. And she smiled.

RICH MERCHANT: How can you tease me at a time like this? I'm really worried.

POOR MERCHANT: Tease you? Didn't I agree with you that strange things happen? After all, if mice can eat up my stock, maybe eagles can fly away with children!

Child comes running out. Mother hugs her.

RICH MERCHANT: Forgive me, please. I deserved that fright. Come over to my house for supper and I'll give you every penny of the profit I made from selling your stock. I'm truly sorry for being so greedy.

NARRATOR   And after that the two merchants really became good neighbors.

Both return to shop fronts, and child helps out both with customers.

RICH MERCHANT: Why don't you go next door? She's got the best cookware in town and at a really good price too.

POOR MERCHANT: I don't stock cutlery. Just go next door to my neighbor. She'll help you and give you the best price in town.

NARRATOR: So both of them lived and worked happily side by side and stayed the best of friends.

Activities to Use with *Good Neighbors*

Discussion

Students can talk about different kinds of buying and selling, ranging from garage sales and flea markets to corner stores and huge supermarkets.

The market of *Good Neighbors* is very similar to Saturday morning "farmers' markets" which are held both inside and outdoors. Students may compare different kinds of shopping experiences, such as how various customers behave at a sale.

Actors need to observe everything and everyone around them. Students should observe and record what they notice about people who buy and sell in different environments. A trip to an open-air market would be ideal. Observing street vendors would also be useful.

The class's observations about behavior and the different uses of voice and attitude at slow and busy times in the marketplace should provide some interesting information.

Role play

Students may illustrate, in pairs or small groups, different styles of buying, selling, complaining about products and prices, and comparison shopping.

Reading

"The O-Kay Store" from *Raisins and Almonds*, by Fredelle Bruser Maynard (Penguin, 1985). This story tells of the struggle to keep a small family store afloat during the Depression, in the face of the new "Bargain Emporium" and anti-Semitism in a prairie town.

Students may share incidents of a similar nature, or of discrimination, then dramatize the incidents and discuss possible solutions to such problems.

What is fair and unfair competition?

Many corner stores are run by immigrant families, and are often squeezed out by giant foodstores. Could this be relevant to the play?

In small groups of four to six, ask students to improvise on the following topics: "breaking a trust"; "telling a lie". Then ask them if a lie is ever justified. Groups may improvise incidents to illustrate their views.

Voice and text

Students sell the group or class an idea — for example, persuading them about the merits of a book or movie they have enjoyed, or persuading them *not* to see or read something.

In this exercise, everyone will likely pay attention. Ask students to try to capture attention in a more competitive environment, such as outdoors at recess.

In the play, the merchants need to compete verbally against each other. Ask three people to stand on chairs or desks. Tell them they will each be selling an imaginary item and must persuade the rest of the group to buy. They will be speaking and using selling techniques simultaneously, and should keep going as long as possible. Class members should move to whichever "salesperson" is the most interesting. This is *not* a popularity contest, but will underline what is required of the merchants. All the students should have a turn at making a sales pitch. In an ESL classroom, other language use may be appropriate to instill confidence in drama. Students may speak in the language they feel most comfortable with.

Concentration

In the play, the rich merchant must be able to tell a lie without giving herself away; in small groups, students should take turns in telling a "big lie" with as much conviction as possible (and without laughing!).

Characterization

The play gives many clues as to the kind of people the two rival merchants are, but being a customer can be a good opportunity to try out being any of several different people. Students should be encouraged to answer the question "Who am I?" (For example, a tired secretary on her way home wants a cup of tea but broke her favorite mug this morning. It's the end of the week and she only has a couple of dollars left. What will she do? Or two friends are browsing for a bargain. What is their relationship? What will draw their attention?)

Students should ask themselves. "Why am I in the market at this particular time?" "Do I usually buy from one or other of the merchants?" "Would I do anything for a bargain?" Crowd work can be fun and important if students are challenged as much as if they had a large speaking role.

Customers may be of many different nationalities. Students can investigate some everyday occurrences in a store that have dramatic possibilities. What happens, for instance, between a store clerk, a grandmother, and a grade-school child who must interpret for the grandmother? Or have the students improvise a misunderstanding between clerk and customer, or an interaction with one or more customers.

The poor merchant in the play is treated badly. Groups of three to six may work on a scene in which one person is discriminated against for reasons of difference — poverty, dress, color, religion, etc. They should explore both the problem and the outcome in their scenes, and then discuss the results.

Speaking while working

Students will need lots of practice at speaking the text while busy dusting, arranging goods, cleaning, or sweeping. It takes such practice to do more than one thing at a time. In pairs, students should mime an activity while speaking about something else. This is an excellent practice activity for ESL students.

Speaking in the third person

The technique of each character describing his own actions may be unfamiliar to the students — e.g., " 'She'll never be back,' she said to her child. "

Ask students in groups of three or four to take it in turns to describe some simple event that happened recently, but give the story in the third person, saying "She left the house" instead of "I left the house", etc.

Narration

In groups, have students create a far-fetched story like that about the "mice gnawing up the pans". They may compete for a "most outrageous" award.

The Pied Piper of Hamelin

Cast

This play is designed for a class of twenty-five or more. With careful double casting (councillors / rats / children), it is possible to reduce the size to sixteen or even fewer. Lines may also be reapportioned.

PIED PIPER *Male / Female*
NARRATOR *Male / Female*
RATS (1 - 5) *Male / Female*
MAN 1 *Male*
MAN 2 *Male*
WOMAN 1 *Female*
WOMAN 2 *Female*
WOMAN 3 *Female*
MAYOR *Male / Female*
COUNCILLORS (1 - 5) *Male / Female*
LAME CHILD *Male / Female*
CHILD 1 *Male / Female*
CHILD 2 *Male / Female*
CHILD 3 *Male / Female*
CHILD 4 / CAT *Male / Female*
CHILD 5 / DOG *Male / Female*
PARENTS *(Man 2 and Woman 3)*

Staging

The play works well in any kind of staging — full round, horseshoe, or proscenium.

The only essential "scenery" are the hill and the river. The hill can be built up with tables, chairs, or large boxes covered by a cloth. It can be represented by a curtain across a half-open door (freestanding or the classroom door). Even a blackboard or an easel covered with paper works well, as do screens or partitions.

The river may be a long piece of cloth attached at one end to a part of the set. The rats may disappear under the cloth.

The full cast may be present throughout and freeze when not required, or the politicians may enter and exit where appropriate in the action.

Props and masks

A flute or bamboo pipe or recorder for the Pied Piper.
River cloth.
Hill drape.
Rat "noses" (inexpensive to purchase and easily obtainable from toy stores) or half-masks of grey felt made out of felt squares from handicraft stores. The masks for the cat and dog may also be made from felt squares and simply painted. Half-masks or half-squares are sufficient.
Paper cut-outs of rats fastened to sticks of dowel are an alternative.
A chain of office for the Mayor.
A riding crop or pointer for the Mayor, to lend authority.
A cane or crutch for the lame child.

Costumes

Pied Piper: A red and yellow tie-dyed top, with a long cotton scarf. Bright pants or tights.

Councillors: Normal "uniform"-type clothes, all khaki, or navy and military-style berets.

Rats: Black gloves or mittens — grey or black T-shirts and pants. Bare feet or dark sneakers.

People/Children: Bright clothes — contemporary.

Mayor: As councillors, but with chain of office.

The Pied Piper of Hamelin

Adapted from Robert Browning's
narrative poem of the same name

When the play opens the people of the town of Hamelin, their children and pets, are frozen in various attitudes of work, play, or rest. The narrator steps forward to introduce the play.

NARRATOR: This story is about broken promises, and what happened to a town that broke its word.
      Long ago, the country town of Hamelin, which stood on the banks of a large river, was overrun by a plague of rats.

The rats, who have been concealed amongst the audience, now enter the playing space. They run, jump, squeak, etc., and are a thorough nuisance; during this activity the narrator steps back and the tableau of townspeople comes to life.

RAT 1:   They fought the dogs,

A fight is staged between one of the rats and dogs, and between a rat and a cat.

RAT 2:   And killed the cats,

RAT 3:   Bit the babies sweet and fat,

RAT 4:   Clawed on clothes,

RAT 5:   And chewed on hats.

NARRATOR: They interrupted talks and chats,

RATS 1-3:   By shrieking

RATS 4-5:   And squeaking

NARRATOR: In notes that ranged from sharp to flat. In fact, they got into everything and made life impossible for the people.

Adults and children in two groups complain simultaneously.

WOMAN 1:   We can't go on like this. I found whiskers in my cake mix!

WOMAN 2:   There was a nest in the flour bin. I counted six!

MAN 1:   I opened my lunch tin, one nibbled the bread.

CHILD 1:   Those rats are the *only* ones getting fed.

CHILD 2:   Oh, how I'd like to sleep on a clean, safe sheet.

CHILD 3:   I hate touching fur with my two bare feet.

During this exchange, the people shoo, brush, and push the rats away — they go back gradually to their original places.

WOMAN 1:   Let's go and complain to city hall.

MAN 1:   They'd better listen or heads will fall.

WOMAN 3:   We all pay taxes, we've a right to our say.

MAN 2:   These kinds of problems won't run away.

ALL: We'll go and see what they intend to do.

NARRATOR: So they went to complain to that lazy crew!

A typical meeting is in progress at "City Hall" (at one end of stage). If rats double as town councillors, they need only remove their masks and put on military-type berets. They lounge around casually.

COUNCILLOR 1: Your Worship, spies tell me the people are angry, they want action, something quite drastic.

MAYOR: Right, got a suggestion? Who's got an idea? You? (*points to councillor 2*) I hope something fantastic!

COUNCILLOR 2: (*who has been half asleep*) Sir, we're thinking, we're doing our best.

COUNCILLOR 3: I know! Put down more poison in every nest.

Meanwhile, the townspeople are standing listening to the council.

COUNCILLOR 4: (*energetically, noticing the crowd*) Let's import foreign cats to fight.

COUNCILLOR 5: That's it! The rats would vanish overnight!

MAN 1:   Find a solution, we won't wait much longer.

WOMAN 3:   Show those creatures who's the stronger!

NARRATOR: Then they went home, with just one thought — somehow those rats had to be caught.

The townspeople return to their designated "homes" and work quietly on a variety of chores.

MAYOR: Let's deal with the problem. Quick — my vacation's due. What are your thoughts?

COUNCILLOR 1: More poison, send out some reports.

COUNCILLOR 2: Find someone to invent a new kind of trap.

COUNCILLOR 3: (*yawning*) I can think better *after* my nap!

MAYOR: There's no doubt this task is tough.
             I'll offer a reward, there's gold enough!

A loud knocking is heard.

MAYOR: Who's there? We're in a meeting, can't be disturbed.
             These interruptions must be curbed!

Enter the Pied Piper, a striking figure in red and yellow carrying a musical pipe.

NARRATOR: The stranger walked in with a nod for a greeting.

PIED PIPER: Forget your meeting.
I can help you with a secret charm
I use on creatures that do people harm:
All those that live beneath the sun
Who creep or swim or fly or run
Must follow me, cannot return,
Whether they're toads, bats, or poison viper,
And people call me the Pied Piper.

MAYOR: If you can really clean up the town, we'll pay you anything you ask.

COUNCILLORS: It's a terribly difficult task.

MAYOR: We beg you put the rats away.

ALL: We all promise to pay.

PIED PIPER: My fee is $1,000, are you agreed?

MAYOR: I'd pay twice that. (*they shake hands on the deal*) You have our word, it's what we need.

The councillors and the mayor congratulate each other at their good fortune. Freeze. If councillors are doubling as rats, they now put on masks.

NARRATOR: The Pied Piper lifted the pipe to his lips and began to play, and as the third note died away. . . .

People run and watch in amazement as the rats come from different directions.

MAN 1: Fat rats, skinny rats, ugly, slow, how many I can't tell.

WOMAN 1: They're coming from every hide-out to follow the piper's spell.

MAN 2:   Ugh, that one fell out of my sleeve.

WOMAN 2:   I can't believe they'll really leave.

WOMAN 3:   Look at them now, how they're running faster,
             following the music of their master.

NARRATOR: He led them to the river outside the town,
             the water parted and swallowed them down.

*Rats follow the Piper under the river cloth and behind the hill.
If the councillors and rats have been double-cast, the "rats" may now
remove their masks, don hats, and join the people in rejoicing.*

ALL: In joy the people cheered and sang.

CHILDREN: The children shouted and the church bells rang.

NARRATOR: The mayor ordered every rat hole to be boarded up so that
             they could never return.

Everyone helps in the clean-up. The Pied Piper re-enters.

PIED PIPER: It seems my work is finished here,
             I've rid you of the rats you fear.
             $1,000 was the sum I heard
             You offer; pay up please and keep your word!

*The mayor and the councillors turn away to consult. Isolated phrases such
as "I can't start a precedent", "Impossible", etc. are heard. All look at
the mayor.*

MAYOR: You misunderstood, we spoke in jest.
             Those rats were such a filthy pest!
             Take half the cash, put out your hand,
             We've huge expenses, *you* understand!

PIED PIPER: I don't! That charm you ordered you may keep,
             But magic you'll find does not come cheap.
             Pay up, or the next tune I play
             Will give you cause to regret this day.

MAYOR: Don't threaten us, you patchwork clown!

COUNCILLOR 1: Who cares? We saw the rats go down.

COUNCILLOR 2: Indeed, we all saw those vermin sink.

MAYOR: And the dead don't come to life, I think.

All the council laugh at their mayor's wit, encouraging him to defy the Piper.

MAYOR: Play all you like, play until noon,
            You'll get nothing from us for that silly tune!

NARRATOR: Then the Pied Piper lifted the flute to his lips one more
            time. Too late now to repent the crime.

Piper plays.

MAN 1:   Wherever the children happened to be
            They left their toys and came to see

WOMAN 2:   What magical music that could be.

*The children start to move towards the Piper after the third note and gather
around him. He leads them slowly around the acting area, then speeds up
and moves towards the hill.*

MAN 2:   They moved so fast, and no one waved.

WOMAN 3:   Of all those kids, just one was saved.

*The children speak almost simultaneously as they skip, run, and crowd
around the Piper. The lame child starts to follow the others and walks very
slowly, sometimes having to rest.*

CHILD 1:   It's holiday music.

CHILD 2:   It reminds me of the taste of ice cream.

CHILD 3:   I think there will be ponies where we're going.

The Pied Piper of Hamelin   23

CHILD 4:   And elephants and clowns and jugglers.

CHILD 5:   I'm going to join the circus.

ALL: No more school.

PARENTS: Stop them, he's stealing our children.

MAYOR: They'll stop at the hill, it leads nowhere.

At that moment the Piper turns and sounds one long note, and the adults in the village freeze, unable to reach the children by voice or movement.

LAME CHILD: Wait, I can't go so fast, I want to come with you.

NARRATOR: Then the Pied Piper's spell opened the hill and they disappeared, voices heard still.

Children disappear behind hill.

CHILD 1:   It's sparkling with fireworks.

CHILD 2:   Look at the grapes, and the toys.

CHILD 3:   And birds — I've never seen such bright ones!

As the last child exits the people become unfrozen.

MAYOR & COUNCIL: Wait, don't go, it was all a mistake.

PARENTS: We love you, come back for our sake.

NARRATOR: But the children were gone, the hill closed forever, and nothing would ever be the same again. It was too late.

LAME CHILD: Wait, please wait!

The lame child reaches the hillside and beats on it. It is futile. He or she leans against the hill and faces the audience now.

LAME CHILD: They ran inside the hill too fast,
I couldn't catch up, I'm always the last.
The music has stopped, and I am here still,
Without my friends, locked out of the hill.
We'll never play like we did before,
I'll be alone forever more.

NARRATOR: Then he limped back to his parents, forlorn.
The town searched for the Piper, but he was gone.

MAYOR: I'll offer a reward. Go at full speed!

Everyone is silent and just looks at the mayor. He removes his chain of office and says quietly:

MAYOR: I lost my child too, I'm sorry for my greed.

LAME CHILD: No one came back. The street was renamed the "Pied Piper's Street" and a sign was put up for visitors to read,

NARRATOR: About the town that broke its word, a town without children
Where grown-ups wept,
For a promise is a promise and must be kept.

Activities to Use with
The Pied Piper of Hamelin

Discussion and text research

1. Broken promises to members of the class, and/or by class members themselves.

2. Circumstances that might make a broken promise acceptable.

3. The original poem by Robert Browning was written more than a hundred years ago, but the actual story is more than five hundred years old. How modern, or relevant to the present time, is the core of the drama? This can be discussed in the light of recent political events in the world.

4. What do students understand by an "election promise"? After recent local or national elections, how many politicians' promises were actually kept?

5. The townspeople in the play confront their politicians with their grievances. Students should research similar occurrences in their own country. Possible topics include indexing of pensions, closing of rail lines or factories, etc. What might happen in a non-democracy? Their answers must be based on textual evidence, such as research in newspapers and other publications, or radio and TV reports.

6. Groups decide on the best wording for the sign that was put up in Hamelin to tell about the terrible events. The whole class then decides which wording to use.

Acting and storytelling

1. In pairs students improvise different types of complaints:
(a) Complaining over the telephone to the head of a big business.
(b) Complaining by parent and teacher about student/teacher attitude.
(c) Complaining by friends in a school corridor or playground about their lives, each one trying to prove that their life is the worst.
   In each case, students should reverse roles after finishing the scene.

2. In pairs and groups, students work on scenes of saying goodbye in different circumstances — children going off to the crusades, or to another war; children going to summer camp; children going overseas by themselves to visit relatives; children running away and leaving notes.

Students should take note of the differences between a voluntary departure (both sides agree), an involuntary one, when only one of the two sides is in favor, and one in which no one wants anyone to leave.

3. In this play there are often several things going on at the same time — e.g., there is a fight between the animals while other people are on stage working and playing, and the council meeting goes on while the crowd watches and listens. Students may improvise scenes where two groups are on stage simultaneously. While one group is active, the second group must be present and involved without taking away the audience's attention.

Making demands as a group

(Group sizes may vary from three or four in younger classes to ten or twelve in more experienced ones.)

1. Demand better working conditions from an employer. (The group will decide on the kind of work and select a leader, but not rehearse the outcome.)
2. Demand a raise, and give reasons for and against.
3. Demand an investigation into crooked practices of any kind of organization.
4. Demand better treatment of animals in a local hospital, zoo, circus, etc.

Other groups should watch and then discuss approaches that may be incorporated into the production.

Individual work

Students are asked to imagine they are competing for an important position — president of a club, a promotion at work, etc. They must make a speech outlining their special qualities in order to get what they want.

Characterization

In a play with a large cast and crowd scenes, it is important to make the people believable. Each cast member needs to search the script and stage directions for clues as to the character he or she should be, then fill in "gaps" by deciding on the age, occupation, likes, dislikes, and kind of person he or she is portraying. How would the character react to the situations in the play?

Text and improvisation

After the play has been read aloud to/by the class two or three times, it may be acted out in the class's own words. Is the rhyme helpful, or do the actors prefer their own prose version? They may discuss why the poetry might be important to the style of the play.

Unison speech

There are several instances where characters are asked to speak in unison. Various ways of doing this may be tried — either as one voice, or by overlapping words, or ignoring the direction and dividing the lines among players. The cast should use whatever method works best for the production.

Movement

Students should look at pictures of rats, or observe one in a pet shop or at home, then create their own movement vocabulary of rat-like actions. A decision must be made as to whether rats will walk on all fours or whether a stylized movement will be used, walking upright but with rat-like actions.

Before-and-after scenes

1. Groups of four or five improvise family scenes both *before* the children leave and *after* they have gone, when the townspeople return to their empty homes.
2. Groups improvise the first council and public meeting *after* the departure of the children.
3. Groups improvise any part of the play, but remove it to another setting. For example, the town councillors might be gang leaders in Prohibition times.
4. One rat survives, escapes, and "tells" of his ordeal to rats in another town.

Further topics for dramatic interpretation

At the end of his poem, Robert Browning writes of a remote Transylvanian tribe of alien people who are proud of their outrageous dress, and who, it is said, are the descendants of people who emerged from a cave or "subterranean prison" after being led from their homes by a mysterious Piper, for unknown reasons.

Students could work on any aspect of the poem or play: the children when the hill closes behind them and they are inside the cave; how and why they get out; their organization and adaptation to a world outside; story-telling of how life was long ago.

Do rats have rights?

The following article is from the *Vancouver Province* of 7 January 1990. Students may choose any part of it to dramatize or discuss.

A Vancouver artist who had planned to crush Sniffy the rat had to run for his life yesterday.

An angry crowd of more than 300 gathered outside Vancouver Public Library, where Gibson was to drop a 25-Kilogram block of concrete and capture the event on canvas.

Animal rights activists carrying signs reading: "Killing is not art." and "Rats have rights." lay in wait for Gibson outside the Vancouver Public Library.

Gibson appeared at 1 p.m. without rat or rat-killing contraption, to tell the crowd: "I no longer have Sniffy. I have returned him to the pet store I rented him from.

"If people are still concerned with saving Sniffy, they can go to the pet store and get him. Maybe now as I speak, he's being purchased by someone to be fed to a snake in their terrarium."

Rats, one encyclopedia tells us, "rank among the most serious animal threats to people." They carry the germs of diseases, including typhus, and cause billions of dollars of property, crop and livestock damage every year. Domestic rats indulge our own need to kill — they are used primarily for experimentation or, as Gibson kept pointing out, fed live to pet snakes.

We would have been sickened had Gibson killed Sniffy. But how far would people have gone to protect this rat? And it is surely amazing that a rat under a silly death threat gets as much notoriety as the millions of children who starve to death every year. Gibson gave us much to talk about, think about and question. And that surely is a hallmark of art.

The Party

Cast

The cast size is flexible — as few as seven or as many as fifteen. This play is ideal for an all-girl group.

NARRATORS 1 & 2 *Male / Female*
AEI *Female*
CHANTRA *Female*
KOOMPANG *Female*
RATTANA *Female*
PEN *Female*
AEI'S MOTHER *Female*
SEVEN VILLAGE GIRLS *(These may be double-cast.) Female*

Staging

A variety of options, ranging from an empty space in which everything is mimed, to painted backdrops or screens and multi-levels such as risers to denote the settings of village, forest, river, and mountain.

Shadow play

An alternative would be to set up as though for a shadow puppet play, with a backlit sheet or paper screen.

Each character would be double-cast. The voices or chorus would stand at the side of the stage, the actors acting out the words behind the sheet, lit from lights above and behind them.

Props and costumes

Many or none, depending on the concept of your production. If costumes are used they might reflect Thai culture.

Lighting

Day, evening, and night are part of the play, and if used, lighting could indicate this. Colored gels for the forest, water, and mountain would also be effective. No lights are really necessary, but some technical possibilities are suggested for classes who want to experiment with them.

The Party
Based on a legend from northern Thailand

NARRATOR 1: Long ago, maybe as long as 1,000 years ago, there were two villages separated from each other by a small mountain.

In the evening, when their work was finished, the girls from both villages took turns to visit each other, or met on the mountain.

NARRATOR 2: Their parents complained that they were never home and were always wasting their time. No one took any notice. Parents have complained about their silly daughters for as long as anyone can remember.

NARRATOR 1: There was very little news for the girls to talk about, so they would complain about the weather. . .

GIRL 1: How hot it was today! I'm worn out from gathering the harvest.

GIRL 2: It was so hot today, I could have drunk the river dry.

GIRL 3: I had to carry the rice out to the workers, and I nearly dropped dead from the heat.

GIRL 4: You're lucky you got to go outside. I had to watch the babies, and they screamed all day!

NARRATOR 2: Often they would gossip about each other.

GIRL 5: I heard Aei has another new dress. She just twists her parents around her little finger.

GIRL 6: Do you think Pen's new hairstyle suits her? I wish my mother would let me try something different.

GIRL 7:   I'm sure Rattana likes that new worker of Sumlee. You
               should have seen the looks she gave him at the meeting.

*The gossiping, giggling, and whispering may be continued and improvised
along similar lines, if desired.*

CHANTRA: I'll go mad if we don't talk about something new.

PEN: Never mind talking, let's do something new. How about
               a party on Friday night?

KOOMPANG: What about running races down the hill with the girls from
               the next village?

Everybody groans.

PEN: You'll suggest fishing next!

AEI: But we've had parties before. What would be so special
               about this one?

RATTANA: Yes, it'll just be the same faces, same talk — boring!

PEN: Then we'll make it different. Why don't we all dress up?

CHANTRA: Yes! And we'll give a prize to the most beautiful girl!

AEI: Oh, of course. Look who's got the longest, blackest hair.
               Come on, Chantra, that's not fair!

RATTANA: I agree. We don't all have big dark eyes like Koompang.

CHANTRA: Or slim ankles like me!

Laughter.

PEN: I know, let the prize be for the most wonderful looking
               outfit, as well as looks. Everything will count.

AEI: Let's do it!

The cast move to various places around the acting space. Each girl has her own pile of costumes/props. Each speech should be followed rapidly by the next one, so that there is minimal pausing between monologues. If lighting is used, each girl could be in a special pool of light while speaking, others remaining frozen and in shadow until it is their turn.

KOOMPANG: I'll wear my new skirt and put a ribbon in my hair, and I'll thread red beads for an anklet the way Chantra showed me.

PEN: I'll braid my hair a new way, with flowers, and tuck a flower in my belt too.

RATTANA: I wonder if Mother will lend me her new shawl if I tell her it's for something really special. . . (*tries it on*) Oh, it looks wonderful! I know she'll say yes!

CHANTRA: A blue sash, and blue slippers. Maybe I'll shorten my skirt just a little too.

AEI: (*wails*) I don't know what to wear.

The biggest pile of clothes is in front of her.

I know they've all made up their minds already. They've been planning all week. I think they're jealous of me. I must win! Oh, how can I choose? (*calls*) Mother, please come and help.

Mother enters carrying a long blue scarf.

Mother, do you think I'll be more beautiful if I wear this ring with *this* bracelet with this skirt, or would the brown one be better — oh no, not brown, red maybe, or what about this hat and this shawl?

MOTHER: You always look lovely in anything, but I think blue is best for you. Wouldn't you like to borrow this blue scarf? You could wear it for a sash 'round your waist.

AEI: Oh no, I think one of the other girls is wearing blue.

MOTHER: Then how about your pink blouse? I've just washed it for you.

AEI: Mother, I'm not a baby; no one wears pink anymore.

MOTHER: Well, your green dress is nice, and you can match it with a green and gold necklace. Pen would help you make one.

AEI: Mother, don't you understand? It's a competition. If I ask Pen, she'll tell the others, and they'll know what I'm wearing and find something better. You're never any help! And besides, everyone has seen all my things.

Mother tries to sort through the pile of things and tidy up.

AEI: Please leave me alone, don't touch my things! Oh, I've just got to be the best.

MOTHER: I think you're feverish. Maybe you'd better stay home tonight. Let me feel your forehead.

AEI: No, please let me go. I'm just nervous about looking right. I'm sorry I was impatient. I'll tidy up.

MOTHER: Very well then, but don't be late, and hurry up now. I can hear your friends outside. (*exiting*) She gets too excited about these things. It's time those girls did something useful with their spare time.

VOICES OUTSIDE: Isn't she ready yet? I love the blue. Hurry up, Aei, or we'll leave without you. What are you doing in there? I wish my mother would let me buy so many clothes.

Meanwhile Aei is putting on all the clothes she owns, one on top of the other. The result should be to make her look fat and grotesque. Her friends look at her in astonishment and try to stifle their giggles. They begin to walk to the mountain.

PEN: What a wonderful disguise, Aei, but won't you be too hot?

AEI: Don't walk so fast, I can't keep up with you.

KOOMPANG: How did you manage to wear so much?

CHANTRA: We'll never get there. Take something off — you're going to roll down the mountain like a fat little squirrel.

AEI: Don't be so rude! I couldn't make up my mind what to wear, so I put on everything (*puffing and out of breath*) I own. I can't get up the mountain like this. Let's go through the forest.

The others run ahead and Aei waddles slowly after them.

RATTANA: Doesn't she realize how ugly she looks like that?

KOOMPANG: What a joke! She can't be serious.

PEN: See you later. We'll tell the others you're on your way.

NARRATOR 1: And the girls disappeared into the forest, which was a short cut to the next village.

NARRATOR 2: Aei tried to follow, but her clothes caught on the brambles and tree branches scratched her face.

AEI: (*calls*) Don't start the competition without me! Help! I'm stuck, come and get me!

Voices off. Laughing and chattering.

GIRLS: See you at the party. Bye.

AEI: It's no use going this way, I'll try the other way across the stream, that's even quicker. (*stumbling*) Ouch! I should never have come this way.

Aei backs out of the imaginary forest and continues her journey till she comes to the stream.

NARRATOR 1: She reached the big flat stepping stones and started to cross, but what was usually a simple journey ended that day in disaster.

Aei loses her balance and, with a shriek, falls into the "water".

AEI: Oh, my feet are all wet, and now my beautiful skirt is muddy, I'll be so late. I'll just have to struggle up the mountain. I hope this mud will brush off. I want to win so much!

NARRATOR 2: So Aei slowly began to climb the mountain. Suddenly more of her friends appeared.

The girls pull her along.

GIRL 1: We're late for the party.

GIRL 2: We saw this fat old woman puffing up the hill.

GIRL 3: But it was you! What a disguise! Fantastic!

GIRL 4: Did you think it was a costume party?

GIRL 5: We'll give you a big push, fatty.

AEI: Stop teasing, you're all just jealous, and don't pull so hard — you'll crease my clothes, and your hands are dirty too.

GIRL 6: Dirty! That's the thanks we get for helping you. We're off.

GIRL 7: Climb the rest of the way yourself. You look ridiculous.

The girls walk on.

NARRATOR 1: And so Aei was left on the mountain. It was getting quite dark now; she stumbled and slipped along; her wet skirts got in her way. Suddenly she tripped over a rock and fell, down and down to the bottom of the mountain, without a sound.

Aei rolls and tumbles across the acting space.

NARRATOR 2: When her friends returned home from the party they found Aei's dead body. Sadly they lifted her up and carried her home.

NARRATOR 1: There were no parties in the two villages for a long time.

NARRATOR 2: The name the village gave to the hill was "Neun Sao Aei", which means, "The girl who wore too much". A stone pagoda was built where Aei died, and her friends used to sit there and remember her. It stands there still.

Activities to Use with
The Party

Discussion

1. "Disguise". What do students mean by the word? A fashionable pair of sunglasses may be just as much a disguise as full face make-up. The discussion may include occasions such as Hallowe'en when a costume is required, theatre disguises (make-up and clothes to create a character on stage), traditional occasions that demand the ritual wearing of a special outfit (e.g., weddings, funerals, school graduations, etc.), and all kinds of uniforms.

The discussion should move on to changes in behavior that result from the kinds of outfits worn. A police officer, for instance, is expected to reflect the image his or her uniform provides, and the public perceives the officer accordingly.

Students may illustrate their ideas by talking about their own clothes — e.g., "designer" clothes — and wearing clothes that identify one as a member of a group, trying to make an impression on the first day of school, etc. Do people make immediate judgments based on appearance?

2. Is *The Party* a play just about clothes? What else do the students feel it is concerned with?

3. Does the girl Aei have a modern counterpart? Are there people who think only about their appearance?

4. This story is based on a Thai legend. Are there any aspects of it that could be true today? What scenes can students identify with? What aspects of the story are sexist?

5. How are humor and sadness contrasted in this story? What different kinds of humor are used?

Improvisation

1. With partners, students improvise the following conversation between a "parent" and "child". The opening lines are:
    "I've got nothing to wear for the party on Friday."
    "I'd prefer you not to go anyway."
    After acting out a scene, they reverse roles.

2. "Shopping spree." Three friends each have a certain amount of money to spend, and have to put together an outfit for a special occasion. The improvised scene must contain at least one thing that changes the course of events. For example, one girl phones home and discovers her single mother has lost her job. What differences of attitudes towards each other, the spending of the money, and their own images do this girl and the others discover?

3. "Nothing to do." Divide the children into groups of five or six. Their dilemma is that they are friends who live in a very small community without shops or entertainment of any kind. The group decides to liven things up. How?

4. Monologues. Students write and perform their own monologues about clothes (e.g., "I always wanted to look like my friend", or "I hate the way some people dress"). If a video camera is available, the speeches could be played back and commented on.

5. Groups of six to eight mime activities in different locations, such as a forest, beach, farm, or store. Then they freeze one moment of activity that seems the most site-specific. Groups watching should be able to recognize the setting.

6. Students devise a short play with a situation similar to that in *The Party*. Is it necessary for the central figure to die? Students may add scenes to illustrate their point or change the ending if they wish.

Earth, Fire, and Water

Cast

NARRATOR *Male / Female*
WIDOW *Female*
HER FOUR CHILDREN:
LI 1 *Male*
LI 2 *Male*
LI 3 *Male*
MOON LI *Female*
VILLAGE WOMAN 1 *Female*
VILLAGE WOMAN 2 *Female*
VILLAGE WOMAN 3 *Female*
VILLAGER 1 *Male / Female*
VILLAGER 2 *Male / Female*
GHOST *Male / Female*
MANDARIN *Male*
TIGER *Male / Female*
SOLDIERS *(at least eight) Male / Female*
MUSICIAN *Male / Female*

Staging

The cast remain on stage throughout the play, sitting or standing as appropriate in a half-circle upstage, and making their entrances and exits from there. Any props or costume pieces such as masks may be placed on stage, in front of or behind the actors, and picked up just before an entrance.

Set

One square riser, if desired, centrestage, to become the house, the cage, the fire, the boat, etc.
A foot stool.

Props

Half- or one-inch thick pieces of wood/bamboo doweling about four feet long (whatever number is required).
 These are carried by the Mandarin and the soldiers, and are transformed

into swords, hunting implements, bars of the prison cage, the fire, oars, boat masts and sides. They are as versatile as the actors want to make them.

Red and orange rags or pieces of cloth to tie to the staves to represent fire. Blue cord or string for the river. If string is tied between two dowels, they may be held high to symbolize the river, and lowered for "the swallowing of the water", then raised again for the return of the river and the drowning.

A set of dice.

Masks

Tiger.
Ghost.
(These may also be rendered with face make-up.)

Costumes

VILLAGERS: Simple cotton tops and pants of sombre colors. The Li children should be dressed identically and wear soft cotton caps. The soldiers are dressed alike, in a plain style similar to that of villagers.

MANDARIN: A bright sash or coat over the basic outfit.

NARRATOR: The narrator is dressed like the villagers.

MUSICIAN: The musician is dressed like the villagers.

Musical instruments

Bells, drum, triangle, or any percussion instrument.

Earth, Fire, and Water
Adapted from a Chinese legend

The cast stand in a half-moon shape to frame the acting space. They remain there throughout the play, coming into the acting area when needed and returning to this space at the end of each sequence. The narrator may have a stool close to the audience. One square riser/platform (*optional*) stands centre.

Scene 1: The village

NARRATOR: Long ago in a poor village called Dragon Pool in the Province of Gensu, in China, the people were afraid of their ruler. Imprisonment and death were a part of everyday life, and no one knew from moment to moment who would suffer next. Life was cheap.

A widow lived there with her four children, who all looked like each other.

They come forward.

MOON LI: Mother, why must I dress like my brothers? People will think I'm a boy.

WIDOW: Because it is safer so.

LI 1: I am the eldest son, Li 1.

LI 2: I am the second son, Li 2.

LI 3: I am the third son, Li 3, and this is my sister, Moon Li.

MOON LI: I have never seen my father. He died when I was born.

She exits upstage and sits apart.

LI 1: He died fighting in the Mandarin's army, against a people he did not know.

Scene 2: Night ghost

Flashback. Moon Li remains turned aside. The rest of the family are grouped centre. The boys are on the ground close to their mother, who holds the new baby (mimed). Village women stand nearby.

WIDOW: I remember the whispers of the women when my daughter was born.

VILLAGE WOMAN 1: A girl child, and four is an unlucky number.

VILLAGE WOMAN 2: The number of death and misfortune.

WIDOW: The day she was born, I remember with sadness her father's death, and I fear for the future.

VILLAGE WOMAN 3: They will surely starve.

WIDOW: We will not go hungry! We will manage to survive. I hold my daughter, the moonlight on her face. I will call her Moon Li.

She whispers the name again. The family sleeps.

NARRATOR: Then out of the walls there appeared a ghost.

The ghost enters to a rustling sound like dry leaves. He stands next to the widow. The children sleep on undisturbed. The widow wakes up, startled, and holds the "baby" more tightly.

WIDOW: Aiaa, Kuei, a ghost!

GHOST: Yes, do not be afraid. On this night, as the soul of your husband leaves this earth and a new soul is born, there is both sorrow and joy. I bring you gifts.

The ghost touches each child gently as he speaks, and a percussion sound accompanies each of his lines. He touches the "baby".

I give you understanding of all things.

He touches Li 3.

>The heat and flame in the heart of the fire will be your friend.

He touches Li 2.

>I give you the strength of the earth, even as my foot stamps on the ground like this (*stamps*).

He touches Li 1.

>The secret of the tides, the ebb and flow of water is yours to know, like your own breath. Use these gifts wisely.

Exit.

Moon Li returns to the family group, and the children now appear as in Scene 1.

Scene 3: The days pass by

LI 1: I fish for our food, I know the river tides. I can empty a pool in one gulp and fill it again with one breath like the torrent from the mountains when the snow melts. No one knows I can do this.

LI 2: I work in the fields with the village oxen, their strength is my strength, and no rock in the ground is stronger than the strength of my arm. No one knows I can do this.

LI 3: I can plunge my hands into the fire and they do not burn. Fire is my friend. The fires I build keep us warm all through the long winter. No one knows I can do this.

Throughout these descriptions the actors mime some of the activities they describe. Boys return to places.

MOON LI: I watch over the sheep and the geese for the village. The animals are my friends.

Scene 4: The ruler

VILLAGER 1: Long days of work, quiet days.

VILLAGER 2: Long days of fear, waiting for the ruler to strike, and his soldiers to threaten.

The Mandarin and his soldiers carrying staves step forward.

MANDARIN: I am the ruler. This is my land and everything upon it belongs to me.

He looks at the people and they bow their heads.

Tonight there will be a banquet to celebrate my victories. Let us hunt.

NARRATOR: And so they set off.

They circle the acting space once.

But the hunt was not for wild game, for the ruler had seen Moon Li with her geese.

Moon Li stands centre. She mimes holding a goose in her arms and stroking its wings.

MANDARIN: Those plump birds will be better than scrawny wild geese. *(he raises his bow)* The boy can do nothing.

Moon Li hears the Mandarin. She raises her arms to let the birds fly and calls and runs in every direction to make the other birds escape. Then she watches them fly away. The Mandarin is angry.

MANDARIN: Seize him and bring him to the cage. I have a very hungry tiger who needs exercise.

Scene 5: Understanding of all living things

Two soldiers seize Moon Li, and led by the Mandarin they walk behind the audience while the remainder of the soldiers set up the prison cage.

They stand in the shape of a square, holding their staves as bars. As soon as Moon Li is thrown into the cage the tiger is led in. A footstool is brought to the Mandarin and he sits and watches in silence. Moon Li stands very still, her eyes on the crouching tiger. Slowly, he stretches and pads once around her, then, with a deep growl, prepares to spring. The Mandarin gets up from his place in his excitement, the people show their feelings in different ways.

VOICE OF GHOST: Understanding of all living things.

The tiger jumps. Moon Li falls to the ground, and suddenly what should have been death becomes play: they wrestle as children do for a moment. Moon Li's laugh and the tiger's purr are heard. She sits on the ground, and the tiger puts his head in her lap and goes to sleep. The soldiers look at the Mandarin for guidance. He is wild with rage.

MANDARIN: Guard the boy well. Tomorrow we will have a public execution!

He makes a sign for the tiger to be led away. Exit.

Scene 6: The strength of the earth

NARRATOR: That night while her mother prayed, Moon Li waited in her cage, but her brothers planned their sister's escape.

The boys sit a little way apart from the prison, and seem to be playing a game of dice. They are waiting for night. As night falls, gradually the soldiers' heads nod in sleep and two slump down to the ground, though their bars are still held upright. The brothers crawl towards the sleeping sentries. One stirs, and Moon Li, watching, stifles a cry. Percussion sounds.

VOICE OF THE GHOST: The strength of the earth.

Li 2 uses all his strength and bends two of the iron bars (pulls the staves apart) so that Li 3 can enter the cage. Quickly he takes Moon Li's place, and she runs to join her mother among the villagers. Li 2 is close by.

Scene 7: The fire

The soldiers wake up and stand to attention as the Mandarin enters.

MANDARIN: Build a great pile of wood and kindling here in the square. The people shall be made to watch one who defies me burn to ashes.

The soldiers step forward. Their wooden sticks are now used to form the fire. They kneel facing inward, and hold the staves together to make a point in the centre. Li3 is placed in front of it. The watching villagers now speak almost simultaneously, and while audience attention is on them, the soldiers tie strips of red and orange cloth to their sticks to symbolize the fire.

VILLAGER 1: Poor woman, to lose her son like this.

VILLAGER 2: Will this cruelty never end?

VILLAGE WOMAN 1: Quiet, or we'll be next. We need not look.

VILLAGE WOMAN 2: If we ignore this, as we have always done, who will be next?

VILLAGE WOMAN 3: May her other children comfort her.

The soldiers move the sticks with their flames, waving them high. They can circle Li3 making it look as if he is being consumed by fire. If he crouches during this sequence, the illusion will be enhanced.

WIDOW: How can he live in those flames?

VOICE OF GHOST: The flame in the fire is your friend.

MOON LI: *(to widow)* We must trust in each other — don't be afraid.

Li 1 now steps behind Li3, the "flames" flicker, then gradually die down. The soldiers effect this by slowly lowering their staves and removing the red rags.

The crowd gasps.

VILLAGERS: Aaii, aiaa!

VILLAGE WOMAN 1: A miracle!

VILLAGE WOMAN 2: He steps unharmed from the ashes!

VILLAGE WOMAN 3: He is a fire ghost!

MOON LI: See, Mother, he is unharmed.

The soldiers turn to the Mandarin for guidance. At that moment Li 3 steps back from his place and is replaced by Li 1. Li 3 mingles with the crowd.

MANDARIN: Seize him! We will take him to the river — man the boat! We will throw him into the deepest part of the Yangtze, and there shall be an end to this defiance.

Two soldiers grab Li 1, while two form the river by holding staves joined by blue cord. The rest arrange their staves into the shape of a boat around the riser. The crowd turns to watch.

Scene 8: The secret of the tides

NARRATOR: When the boat carrying Li 1 reached the middle of the river, the Mandarin spoke.

MANDARIN: Here is the deepest part of the river. The currents are too strong to swim in. Throw him overboard! He shall not survive this time.

The river staves are raised. Li 1 kneels and falls over the side of the boat (a stave held by the soldiers). He is given a push on his way.

VOICE OF GHOST: The ebb and flow of water like your own breath.

NARRATOR: Li 1, who could gulp the river in one breath, opened his mouth and swallowed the water, (*river staves are lowered*) so that the ship capsized and the Mandarin and his men fell in the mud, and slipped and pushed and roared for help. Then Li 1, who had reached the shore, knelt on the river bank and all the water gushed back into the river. (*river staves are raised*)

VILLAGER 1: The waters are rising. They will be drowned!

The villagers cheer.

NARRATOR: And the tyrant and his men were all drowned.

The "river", the Mandarin, and his men leave the stage.

NARRATOR: The people made songs, and in times of trouble they still
whisper them, to get through the bad times.

*In small groups, the villagers (including the Li family) speak the follow-
ing words, underscored by percussion. They are spread in small groups
around the stage, and lines may be apportioned in any way.*

VILLAGERS: We saw from the Yangtze River's banks,
Tyrants whimper as they sank.
The strength of the soil,
The warmth of the flames,
The gift of water will bless our toil,
While Moon Li's compassion our land reclaims.

Activities to Use with
Earth, Fire, and Water

Discussion

1. In what ways could the plight of the Li family be compared to the way some people are still forced to live?

Discussion might touch on the plight of people in the Third World or the role of women in some societies. For instance, Moon Li's mother says it is safer for her to be dressed as a boy. How do students react to this remark? Is it as safe even in our society for girls to be as independent as boys? (Coming home after dark is just one aspect of safety that may be discussed.) Other topics may include political oppression or fighting in an army against a people or in a country that is unfamiliar. These are all topics that are mentioned in the legend and still have relevance.

2. Discuss stories of great strength. Students will be familiar with the story of David and Goliath, and possibly the story of Atlas. Others may be researched, and comparisons among them made.

3. Many stories and legends are concerned with the giving or taking away of gifts at birth. "Sleeping beauty" is a familiar example. If students had the power to bestow three gifts on a well loved child, what would they be? Have each student name three, then write the answers in categories listed on the board — e.g., physical beauty, intellect, wealth, kindness, etc. Then have students narrow down their choice to two, and finally to just one gift. Ask them, "If you could choose one gift for yourself at this moment in your life, something that would truly make a difference to you, what would it be?"

4. Following on from the previous discussion, ask students to list those qualities that they look for in making a new friend. Even if only at an intuitive level, children will be aware that the qualities they seek are not dependent on color or race.

A warm-up game

This exercise enhances quick coordination of thought, movement, and speech. Students stand in a circle and a ball is bounced at random from one participant to another, all around the class circle. Before bouncing the ball, the thrower says "As strong as. . . :" The student receiving the ball must complete the phrase immediately. The game should work as fast as a game of ping-pong. Examples of phrases are "as strong as a horse", "as strong as a tiger". When everyone has had one turn, opposites may be introduced: "As strong as a lion" would be countered by "as weak as a lamb", and so on.

Movement and voice

Students move around the space experimenting with different kinds of movement, ranging from weak or timid to strong and forceful. Walking on tip-toes would be in the weak range, marching or stamping in the strong. All kinds of movements should be tried. During each movement students utter their names in a way that "matches" the movement. They themselves will decide whether a whisper or a shout is right for a particular movement, and the whole vocal range between these levels should be used.

More difficult is to build in *contrast* — e.g., speaking slowly and quietly, but moving firmly and fast at the same time, or crawling and shouting.

Form groups of six to eight. Have them read the play aloud carefully and make a note of every word that describes a different kind of movement. (For example, the tiger pads around, the ghost stamps, Moon Li is seized and thrown into the cage.) Then ask the students to try out these movement expressions.

The next step is for students to realize that there is always a reason for a movement, an objective behind the action.

Ask them to complete the motive for the following sentences:
The tiger pads around the victim in order to. . . .
The ghost stamps the ground in order to. . . .
Moon Li is thrown into the cage because. . . .

Almost always there are two or more people involved. How do those people feel — e.g., the person who is thrown, the ones who must listen and watch?

In groups students may select any short scene in the play, and explore the movement and feelings of the people involved. For example, in Scene 4, Moon Li hears the Mandarin approach and in order to save the geese, whom she loves and protects, she shouts and runs about to make them fly away. Students should explore and experience different roles in the same scene.

Improvisation and acting

1. Examine scenes that show both moral and physical strength. Students will easily be able to identify these from this play and perhaps from others

in this collection. Ask them to build scenes in which, in response to a crisis, characters are asked for both kinds of strength. They may or may not be able to respond to the challenge. A modern example might be a group of hikers, one of whom is badly injured or has fallen into an inaccessible place. There are many decisions to make, each one showing a different kind of courage. Are the hikers involved able to show the kinds of courage needed in the situation? Ask the children to show their scenarios on completion.

2. Students return to the idea of special gifts, and are asked to create original scenes beginning with the line: "I will give you. . ." Groups decide on the gift—e.g., a car, a new attitude, a money-printing machine, the gift of one extra year of life, etc. Each scene must show the difference the gift makes in the lives of the characters, even for one day. In other words, a change must take place.

3. Groups talk about the meaning of the word "escape." One can escape from a dangerous or unhappy situation, such as a train crash or a cruel home. One can escape from a place of confinement (a prison) or escape *to* something. For example, recently East Germans escaped to the West and democracy. Students may decide on the kind of "escape" scene or play they wish to work on, and then narrow down the idea to one short piece of dialogue, which will make the situation clear to an audience. For example:

"We're trapped, I can't open the door."
"Find something to smash it."
"Don't be silly! It's three feet thick."
"Quiet a moment, I hear something."
"And I smell something. They're burning the place."
"We'll never escape."
"How can we warn the town about the smugglers?"
"There has to be a way out."

Students should decide on the number of characters, and who and why they are in this situation. The exercise may identify some playwrights!

4. The play emphasizes the closeness of the family, and brothers and sisters looking out for each other. This is important in any society, but particularly when moving to a new place where friends have not yet been made or in a land where there are economic and political hardships to be faced.

Interesting memories and incidents of sibling support may be shared by students in groups, and archetypical or representative ones acted out. The student whose memory it is should act as director, and give clues as to remembered dialogue, character, and situation. The incidents in the play of one brother substituting for another may have several real-life counterparts.

Mime

Students sit or stand in a circle, and each one creates an object through mime and uses it before "handing" it on to the next student, who transforms it again. Those watching identify the activity: for example, Student One pantomimes holding a bird and ruffles its feathers; when the circle has recognized the activity, the "bird" is passed on. Student Two transforms the "bird" into an activity such as carving a piece of sculpture, or holding a baby.

The play is full of incidents, such as the mother holding her baby daughter, where mime (using the actor's body to create and interact with an object that is not there) is important. Making sure that each piece of mime is accurate and recognizable will help the actors in their performances. For further mime practice, see the activities following *The Talking Fish.*

Further reading as a basis for improvisation

Tales from Gold Mountain, by Paul Yee (Groundwood, 1989). This beautifully illustrated book of Chinese legends told by a Vancouver author is an excellent source for further improvised work.

The Talking Fish

Cast

FISHERMAN *Male*
WIFE *Female*
FISH *(Actor or Puppet) Male / Female*
SERVANTS *(as many as you want) Male / Female*
OCEAN *Male / Female*
WIND, WAVES, AND STORM *Male / Female*
MUSICIAN *Male / Female*

Suggestions for staging

A reversible floor cloth (a painted sheet) to represent the ocean, manipulated by two or more actors, would serve to hide the fish and to be the sea in its different moods.
A small riser or box to represent the rock.
A plain wooden bench to represent the hut.

Props

The old rain barrel: a battered garbage can.
The new rain barrel: a shiny lid on the garbage can.
A large glove fish puppet in bright-colored felt.
A fishing net.
Cotton cloths tied to sticks (like flags) for wind and storm effects.
A new bench, chair, or bench cover to symbolize the new house.
A broom.
A scrubbing brush.
A duster.
A rake.

Costumes

FISHERMAN: Jeans, jacket, or shirt. Cap.
WIFE: Skirt, plain top, an old shawl, and a new one.
FISH: If the fish is played by an actor rather than a puppet, pants or tights and plain T-shirt.
                Mask or face make-up.
WIND/WAVES: See "Props" above.

Musical instruments/sounds

A bucket of water for splash sounds.

A magic sound: a xylophone, kalimba, or any instrument selected by the company.

Alternative: Everything is mimed, and sounds are vocalized.

The Talking Fish

Based on the story of "The Fisherman and His Wife" by the Brothers Grimm

---

Setting: A seashore.

FISHERMAN: On a lonely beach,

WIFE: In a very poor hut,

Actors create the hut by placing a rough bench upstage.

FISHERMAN: There lived a fisherman. . .

They mend a net together.

WIFE: And his hardworking wife.

FISHERMAN: Every day the fisherman went to the shore to catch fish, to eat, and sometimes to sell. . .

WIFE: And his wife waited in their poor hut.

FISHERMAN: Sometimes the net was empty.

BOTH: And then they went hungry.

FISHERMAN: Sometimes the fish were too small to eat, and the fisherman threw them back into the sea.

BOTH: And then they went hungry.

FISHERMAN: One day the net was so heavy, the man could hardly pull it to shore, but when he looked, all he could see was one small fish.

FISH: "Please," said the fish, "throw me back into the ocean to join my friends. You won't be sorry; I can make your life much easier and grant you a wish."

FISHERMAN: The fisherman didn't really believe that, but he was a kind man, and so he threw him back into the water. "Off you go, little talking fish," he said, then picked up his net and went home.

Splash. The musician makes this sound with real water, or vocally.

WIFE: His wife was waiting for him, and as usual she was *not* in a good mood: "Well, do we eat supper tonight?" she said.

FISHERMAN: Her husband replied gently, "The net was empty, except for a small, talking fish, and we couldn't eat something that talks, so I threw it back. He offered me a wish for my kindness.

WIFE: His wife was used to her husband's odd ways, but this was too much for her; "A talking fish and you threw it back? You've gone mad! How could you waste a wish? I'm hungry. Why didn't you ask for a nice crusty loaf of bread? Go back at once and call him."

The fisherman hesitates.

Go on with you.
I won't put up with this behavior one more minute.

FISHERMAN: The fisherman knew he would get no peace and no supper unless he did as he was told, so off he went. He called: "Little fish, little fish, are you there?"

FISH: The fish said, "I'm glad you have returned. Have you thought of a wish?"

FISHERMAN: The man said, "My wife would like a nice crusty loaf of bread for supper, if it's not too much trouble."

FISH: "Go home, my friend," said the fish. "The bread is waiting," and the fish disappeared.

Splash.
Magic sound for wish granting.

FISHERMAN: The man called out his thanks, and then went home and shared the good bread that his wife was eating.

WIFE: The wife had been thinking. She said, "Our rain barrel is falling to pieces. Let's ask the fish for a new one. Well, what are you waiting for? Off you go! Hurry up!"

FISHERMAN: The fisherman walked back to the shore and called quite softly. He hoped the fish would not hear him, for he was ashamed to ask for another favor; he called, "Little fish, little fish, are you there?"

FISH: I see you have returned. Do you need more bread?

FISHERMAN: There is plenty of bread, we thank you, but my wife would like a new rain barrel.

FISH: Go home, my friend. The barrel is waiting for you.

Splash.
A new barrel cover is put in place.
Magic sound for wish granting.

FISHERMAN: When the fisherman got home, he admired the new rain barrel.

WIFE: But his wife wasn't satisfied yet: "I'm tired of living in this old hut," she said. "Go and ask your fish for a fine new house and new clothes, and then I'll need servants to do my work, while I sit and rest and look at the ocean." Then she waited for him to go.

FISHERMAN: Now the fisherman was ashamed to ask for another favor, but his wife had made up her mind! Back he went, and called quietly: "Little fish, little fish, are you there?"

FISH: The fish heard him and said, "What do you want this
                time?"

FISHERMAN: I am sorry to trouble you again, but please build us a new
                house. My wife won't rest until she lives like a fine lady
                with servants to do her work.

FISH: Go, my friend, your wish is granted.

Splash.
*Sound for magic. The new house is created by throwing a bright cloth over
the bench and placing a fine cushion or two on it. Servants appear. The
wife orders them to work. Improvised dialogue. One servant brings her
an elegant shawl.*

FISHERMAN: The fisherman was happy and went home. There was a
                fine house, and servants. Now he could get on with his
                fishing.

WIFE: His wife came to greet him.

FISHERMAN: Well, are you satisfied now?

WIFE: No, indeed, I'm not, this isn't enough; tell your fish that
                I want to be Queen of the Sea and ruler of all the crea-
                tures that swim there.

FISHERMAN: Is there no end to your greed?

WIFE: I will not be satisfied until I rule the seas and the sky too.

The workers freeze at their tasks in horror.

FISHERMAN: Now the man was afraid. This was a terrible thing to ask,
                but he went, for he had always given in to his wife, just
                to keep the peace. As he walked to the shore, the skies grew
                dark and a storm began to rage.

Storm sounds.

FISHERMAN: "Little fish, little fish, are you there?" *(he waits)*

WIND: The wind howled.

WAVES: The waves roared.

FISH: The fish was angry and said, "What do you want this time?"

FISHERMAN: My wife says she wants to rule the sea and the sky.

FISH: This time the fish did not answer. It just disappeared.

Splash.
Magic sound. Storm rages. The new rain barrel is exchanged for the old one, as is the new shawl, and the wife falls down, blown by the force of the wind. The "house" and the servants vanish.

FISHERMAN: I fear our luck has ended. I'll go home and tell that greedy wife of mine that I'm never going to ask the fish for anything ever again.

Storm subsides.

WIFE: The wife picked herself up, for the storm was over, and came to meet her husband feeling sorry for herself. "It is just as it was before. Where is the gratitude of your fish now?"

FISHERMAN: Your greed has made us lose everything. The fish will never come back. Be content with what the sea provides.

BOTH: And they were.

WIFE: Sometimes.

Activities to Use with
The Talking Fish

This is a familiar story in many cultures. The three major roles lend themselves to class work of role exploration in text and spontaneous work.

Discussion

1. The role of the nagging, shrewish, evil wife is common in legend. What other stories do the students know of this type, and what explanation might there be for this kind of stereotyping?
2. After reading *The Magic Sieve* and *The Talking Fish*, students may compare the kinds of greed shown by the sister in the first play and the wife in the second.
3. The granting of wishes is similar to a big Lotto win. Students may discuss whether happiness or unhappiness is the usual result.
4. Ask the students: "If you had one minute to ask for three wishes, what would they be?"
5. This play is similar to the story of "The Three Wishes", in which a husband asks for a pudding, and his wife, angry with him for "wasting" a wish, wishes it would grow on the end of his nose. When it does, the third and final wish must be to get him back to normal. (From *English Fairy Tales* by Joseph Jacobs. Penguin, 1970.) Have students create their own wish granting stories in groups, and then dramatize them.

Warm-up games

1. "A Circle of Wishes". In groups of five or six, students are seated in a circle and pass around a "wish stick" or wand, each making a wish. Each subsequent player must repeat the wish just mentioned, exactly, then add a new one, and so on around the circle. The rule is *exact* repetition, and no hesitation. After a successful round, the game can be tried with everyone making two, and finally three wishes. This is excellent for concentration and memorization. The actual passing of the "wish stick" adds another dimension.
2. "Puppet stories". Any kind of puppet — stick, finger, or glove — is handed around the circle. The first person wearing the puppet establishes the character, mood, and setting of a plot. The story must flow smoothly

and build through complication, crisis, and resolution. Everyone contributes to the story, in role, as the puppet narrator/character.

Acting, improvisation, and text

Any of the following activities may be worked on simultaneously by students or shared in front of the class.

1. Mime
(a) Students work in pairs, taking turns to mime a simple occupation such as sweeping, raking, or planting. Each observer comments on the accuracy and believability of the mime, and suggests less or more detail for clarity.
(b) This time each student adds a mood to the mime, for whatever reason decided on — e.g., pressing a pair of pants for a first day at school, feeling anxious about the occasion. Or shovelling snow angrily because there's a good movie on TV, and your brothers' allowed to watch it.
(c) Finally the actor must incorporate the time of day, suggesting an approximate hour — e.g., oversleeping, brushing teeth, and worrying about being late for a test. Observers should be able to identify three components — action, mood, and time.

2. Talking while doing something else
People do this all the time, doing dishes and chatting about something else, walking and talking. It is more difficult to do on stage. Students can practise in small groups, working on any simple activity and completing it while talking. They should then go to the text, and work on various activities such as net-mending, fish-cleaning, or eating while saying their lines.

3. Domestic arguments
The fisherman's wife nags. What are the causes of her complaint?
(a) In twos and threes students are asked to set up *vocal* arguments between various family members and friends. The subject and the relationship are agreed on first. The class may then comment on whether the relationship and the arguments are clear to the audience.
(b) The exercise is repeated, but this time, during the argument, one party has the upper hand till almost the end; then the balance shifts and the last word goes to the "weaker" partner(s).
(c) In threes. The fisherman and his wife go to a marriage counsellor for advice. This is an opportunity to take on the characteristics of the people in the play, and also to improvise what changes to them are possible.

A fun exercise when rehearsals are getting dull! Roles should be alternated.

4.   Three wishes

The story of "The Three Wishes" is dramatized. Students enact the version of their own choice. (See "Discussion" 5, above.)

Narration

1.   Students are asked to relate a personal incident, but they refer to themselves only in the third person. For example, "She went to the mall and found a wallet", rather than "I went to the mall. . ?" If a mistake is made during the course of the story, the listening group call, "Start again." This is a fun and helpful exposure to the style of story theatre. See also a similar activity for *Good Neighbors*.

2.   In groups of three, students tell the story of the play from the different points of view of the fisherman, the wife, and the fish. The thoughts and words of the characters can be as elaborate and detailed as the narrator wishes, and need not rigidly follow the text.

3.   Groups of five or six decide on a familiar story or nursery rhyme. A narrator tells the story, every word of which is enacted by the group. Whatever word is mentioned, whether hill, ocean, boat, or wall, it must be performed. This is an invaluable exercise for teaching the connection and timing between narrator and actor, and paying attention to what is happening on stage. Groups should perform their plays for each other.

Voice, text, and sound

Students choose a familiar poem or prose text. Then in groups the text is read or spoken by some students while the rest of the group creates sound effects to go with the text. After group exploration and rehearsal, the whole is presented to the class.

The objective is to give practice in an appropriate balance of voice and sound. The exercise is helpful for projection, concentration, and working together to support a speaker. Movement may be added gradually.

The Enchanted Spring

Cast

NARRATOR *Male / Female*
ISRAEL *(boy studying Talmud) Male*
HIS MOTHER *Female*
NEIGHBOR *Male / Female*
EVIL WITCH *Female*
DEMON *(servant to the witch) Male*
BIRD 1 *Male / Female*
BIRD 2 *Male / Female*
BIRD 3 *Male / Female*
VILLAGER 1 *Male / Female*
VILLAGER 2 *Male / Female*
VILLAGER 3 *Male / Female*

MUSICIAN, *who is also responsible for special effects Male / Female*

The play works well with a cast of thirteen or fourteen. With double-casting — e.g., the birds/villagers and the narrator/musician — it is possible to use a cast of eight, or even six.

Should the director wish a female to play the narrator, the only text change necessary would be a slight adjustment in the opening lines, altering the first-person reference.

Staging

The narrator and the musician remain on stage throughout the play, as close to the audience as possible.

There are many ways to present the play, in addition to the total mime concept of "imagination" theatre, where actors create every image and prop through mime.

A set consisting of three stepladders painted black, and a black cube or two for tree stumps, makes an effective design. The ladders may be rearranged by the cast members during the play to suggest trees and the doors of the Ark.

Set design

A piece of rope strung between the ladder serves as a washing line, and indicates Israel's home.

Other options are the use of real tree stumps, a log, and branches in tubs as a symbolic forest.

The spring may be a cloth; tinfoil; paper; or a blue flashlight (colored gel over the light source).

This is also an ideal play to perform outdoors, preferably near water.

Props

Musical instruments: finger bells, a drum or gong, a cymbal, and striker are all possibilities.

A jug.

A "torch" — a short branch of wood with red paper or gel for flame.

Three cut-out birds on doweling sticks, or fixed to garden canes.

If the actors play the birds themselves, half-masks may be used.

Two small rocks or pebbles.

Bubbles.

A washing line.

Clothes in a basket.

A mixing bowl and spoon.

Two rags — one clean, one discolored.

Optional: masks for the demon and the witch, and for the birds.

Costumes

MALE:	Dark pants, collarless shirts, vests, or jackets. Hats or skull caps.
FEMALE:	Shawls, aprons, ankle-length skirts.
WITCH:	Ragged layers, large shawl or top with wide sleeves, or hooded cloak.
DEMON:	Depends on characterization, whether there is an animal element or if he is more human in form. But he should have a ragged appearance.

Being invisible

In the tradition of Asian theatre, when an actor turns facing upstage (or away from the audience) and remains motionless, either standing or crouched, he is invisible to other actors and the audience.

The Enchanted Spring
Based on an Eastern European Jewish tale

The setting is a small village on the outskirts of a forest in Poland, about 150 years ago. As the play opens, the actors playing the birds are facing upstage, frozen. The musician sits beside the narrator. Both are close to the audience, downstage right, throughout the play.

Scene 1. The drought

The narrator moves to a tree stump and picks up a narrow-necked jar which has been concealed behind it. He looks inside, smiles, then comes down to confide in the audience.

NARRATOR: It's still there! *(now speaks to the jug)* Swim, little fish, for that's all you are now, swim for the whole of eternity. Would you believe that once, not so long ago, when I was a boy right here in this village, studying the *Talmud* — the holy writings — this small fish was a fierce demon, conjured up to destroy me and my people?

He replaces the jug and returns to his place, and a boy runs in followed by his mother and a neighbor. The mother and her neighbor are folding up laundry.

NARRATOR: It all started one long, hot summer, twenty years ago.

MOTHER: Israel, where are you going? Have you finished your studies?

ISRAEL: *(speaks while running off, and then sits upstage frozen)* I'm just going into the forest for a while, Mother. It's cooler there.

MOTHER: *(to her neighbor)* The boy studies and dreams; *(calling)* Israel, don't be long, do you hear me? *(shrugs)* So the chickens must wait a little longer.

NEIGHBOR: The chores will get done, they always do. *(fanning herself)* I can't remember a drought this bad. The dogs and the children pant for water.

MOTHER: The well is almost dry. Well, God has his reasons. He'll send rain when the time is right.

The women exit or freeze in the yard.
Israel takes the jug and drinks from the spring, which "flows" near the tree stump.

NARRATOR: That day a miracle occurred, not just finding a pure spring of water when our whole village was gasping with thirst, but a greater miracle yet. Suddenly I heard:

The birds turn to face the audience and begin to speak. Gentle bell sounds under the dialogue.

BIRD 1: I feel sorry for those poor Jews in the village. They pray daily for a rain that cannot fall.

BIRD 2: Are they being punished for wrongdoing?

BIRD 3: Nothing like that. Haven't you heard the witch has made a spell to stop the rain? The clouds cannot form and so everything will die. She's like all witches, terrified of water.

BIRD 2: Can something be done?

BIRD 1: The spell must be broken. The witch wrote the words on a piece of paper, folded it small into an amulet, and buried it under this tree. But no one will ever know the secret.

BIRD 3: If the paper is burned and the ashes scattered over the spring, the spell will be broken. If only we could tell someone!

They exit.

ISRAEL: This is a great miracle! Suddenly I understand the language of the birds as clearly as if it were my own. *(he jumps up quickly)*
   If the amulet is buried here, I'll dig until I find it and do exactly what the birds said. They have secret knowledge of all that goes on in the world.

Hurriedly he digs by a tree stump and soon uncovers the amulet.

ISRAEL: Just as they said, and she did not even bury it very deep. It's locked. I'll break open the amulet on this rock; I dare not look at those unholy words.

He takes out the paper, burns it, and scatters the ashes. This may be mimed. If the actor "shields" the flame, and then seems to throw the ashes into the spring, the audience will accept the symbolic action. Israel looks around from time to time, in case the witch should approach. Bubbles appear as the ashes are scattered. These may be blown by the musician, or by birds, and again a "magical" sound effect of finger bells could be used. Suddenly, Israel looks up eagerly.

ISRAEL: Rain at last! The drought has ended.

Exit.

NARRATOR: So Israel hurried to the house of prayer to give thanks, but he did not intend to tell anyone, in case the power of the spring was used in unholy ways.

Scene 2. The witch and the demon

The witch comes storming to the tree stump. She is very angry.

WITCH: It is not possible! How could rain fall, and yet I saw it with my own eyes! Luckily I was safe from harm in my cave. Someone has found the amulet!

She crouches on the ground and sees the amulet, picks it up, and realizes the paper is gone.

WITCH: Only a mighty wizard could have broken this spell, but who? My revenge will be swift. I cannot let anyone destroy what I create. I will summon my demon servant to listen to the secrets of the forest and I will be avenged.

She makes magical signs, and almost instantly her demon slave appears. She gives him instructions.

> Demon, rise from underground,
> Waste no time until is found
> The spellbreaker who stopped the drought.
> Listen, find him, seek him out.
> And then tell me!

The witch exits, and the demon circles the area and then stops to listen. The demon should give the impression of being able to make himself invisible.

NARRATOR: From all around came the whispering of the birds. It was as if even the trees were speaking of the secret, and of the broken spell.

VOICES: The boy Israel, the boy Israel,

Now like an echo, with magic sounds under the text.

> He broke the spell, witch's spell.
> Rain fell. All is well, well, well.

The demon returns to the witch.

DEMON: I hear it is a youth — Israel — he comes from down there. *(he points in the direction of the village)*

The witch is terrifying in her rage.

WITCH: A boy cannot defy me — I will change him into a sparrow, and you into a hawk to devour him. No! He will be a worm pecked to death by his own chickens. Wait here for my orders.

The witch hurries off.

NARRATOR: And so the witch came to Israel's house and spoke to his mother.

Mother appears holding a mixing bowl and spoon. Cymbal.

Scene 3. The knock on the door

The witch knocks on the "door". As soon as Israel's mother comes face to face with the witch, she knows she is in the presence of something evil. There is a moment of silence as they face each other. The witch speaks, hissing her hatred.

WITCH: I want to see the boy who lives here, Israel.

MOTHER: He is studying at the synagogue.

WITCH: Tell him then, that I know what he has done, and that I have the power to turn him into a stone, as smooth and small as this one.

She caresses a pebble in her hand, suddenly lifts her arm as if to hurl the stone into the distance. The mother holds the bowl tight.

Tell him to keep out of my way, or I will turn him into a stone and drop him into the deepest well in the village. Let him keep away — meddling boy.

Her raised arm drops threateningly. She exits in a fury. Cymbals. Israel's mother stands motionless. Israel returns.

ISRAEL: Mother, what's wrong, what has upset you? Is the cake not rising? What is it? I will see to the chickens right away.

MOTHER: Oh, Israel, I have had a warning. A dreadful thing will happen to you. An old woman was just here. She says she knows what you have done. Tell me what she meant. I know she was a witch; she had the evil eye.

ISRAEL: Mother, I'll tell you everything, but it must be a secret between us. *(he whispers to her)* Tell no one.

MOTHER: You must keep away from her, don't go near the forest again. Promise me, Israel.

ISRAEL: I cannot. But we will trust in God and fear no evil. I'll go now and consult the holy books.

Meanwhile the demon puts a discolored rag in the centre of the "synagogue".

NARRATOR: But when Israel went to the synagogue, a terrible thing had happened. The witch, determined to avenge herself against the Jews, had put a spell on the Ark, the special place where the *Torah* scrolls were kept, and no one could open the doors.

Scene 4. Unclean

The congregation attempt to pull open the doors, but they remain locked, and there are murmurs of fear and dismay as Irael reaches them. The demon stands "invisible", watching.

VILLAGER 1: The Day of Atonement is only three days away, and now we are cut off from the *Torah*'s blessing.

Demon leaves. His work is done.

VILLAGER 2: This must be a punishment for something we have done. Israel, don't just stare, dreaming!

VILLAGER 3: How will we observe the holy days and pray for the departed? This is a very bad sign; let us go home and wait for a sign to tell us what to do.

Israel is left standing alone.

ISRAEL: I must go back to the forest and drink from the spring again. Perhaps I will find out from the birds what has to be done to open the holy Ark.

NARRATOR: A second time Israel dipped the jug in the water and drank from the spring.

BIRD 1: That witch is determined to avenge herself on all the Jews; she can't get her hands on the boy, so the whole village will be punished.

BIRD 3: She had the demon place a rag dipped in the blood of three unclean animals directly beneath the holy Ark. Of course, so long as it remains there, the door must remain shut, or the Bible will be defiled.

BIRD 2: Those poor people think it is their fault, and are afraid they will not be able to worship on the holy days.

BIRD 1: Someone must remove the unclean rag, burn it, and sprinkle the ashes over the spring, then all will be well, for the doors of the Ark will open and the spell will be broken.

BIRD 2: Life is simple if you know where to look and how to listen.

The birds exit.

ISRAEL: Now I must hurry; the holy days are close.

He takes a clean rag from his pocket and hurries to the village. He crawls over the ground and covers the dirty rag placed there by the demon.

NARRATOR: The unclean rag was there, under the Ark, just as the bird had described. So Israel wrapped it up with his clean cloth, never touching the impure one, then ran to the spring, and as before he burned the evil and scattered its ashes.

As the ashes are thrown, bubbles appear over the spring. At the same moment, there is a cheer from the village, where the doors of the Ark have opened. Israel joins the others in celebration and dance. But the demon has returned and seen the unclean rag disappear. He runs to tell the witch.

NARRATOR: And from all around came the whispering of the birds, and again even the trees spoke of the secret and the boy who had defied the witch.

VOICES: The boy Israel, the boy Israel,

Spoken like an echo, with magic sound under the text.

              Israel broke the witch's spell,
              The Ark is open. All is well, well, well.

The demon reaches the witch and kneels low before her on one side of the stage. Cymbal sounds.

Scene 5. Turn him to stone

WITCH: Let your touch turn him to stone,
              Then bring him here, he will atone;
              Deep inside a well he'll lie,
              Denied a breath, a life, a cry.

NARRATOR: So the demon went looking for Israel.

The demon and the witch exit. Israel re-enters opposite.

ISRAEL: I know that the witch will try to destroy me. I will drink
              one more time from the pure spring, and hope that the
              birds will tell me the secrets that they know.

NARRATOR: And for the last time he dipped the jug in the water and
              drank from the spring.

The birds reappear and the magic bells begin.

BIRD 1:   Israel has cleansed the House of God, but because of that
              he is in mortal danger.

BIRD 2:   The demon has orders to turn him to stone; one touch is
              all that it takes, and then the witch will be rid of him forever.

BIRD 3:   And there will be no one to come between the people and
              the evil witch.

BIRD 1:   Perhaps there is still time, for demons fear fire. . .

BIRD 2:	And water too. If the demon is splashed by the pure spring, he will instantly turn into a tiny fish. His choice will be to slave in the heat of Gehenna for a thousand years, or to be food for bigger fish.
BIRD 3:	Witches fear water as we know, and this miraculous spring water could make her disappear.
BIRD 1:	The spring's wisdom can be used three times by a good human being. There is still a chance for Israel to be saved.

The birds fly off.

ISRAEL:	*(calling)* I thank you for your wisdom, birds of the forest.
NARRATOR:	Then Israel made a torch out of a branch and waited, hidden, for the demon.

The demon moves noiselessly, looking around for the boy. He senses his presence, and at that moment Israel jumps out. In his hand is the "burning torch". The demon is now caught between the spring and the fire.

Scene 6. Evil overcome

The demon howls in fear, not knowing which way to go.

ISRAEL:	Take your choice: burn for a thousand years in Gehenna, or be pushed into the spring and die in the belly of a carp.
NARRATOR:	And the demon knew he was trapped.
DEMON:	*(humbly)* Master, I will do your bidding.
ISRAEL:	*(throws a pebble to the demon)* Then throw this stone to your mistress and tell her you have found me. No tricks. I'll be right behind you with my torch.

He also carries the jug of spring water.

NARRATOR:	They reached the witch's cave, and the demon gave the witch the pebble.

DEMON: Here he is.

WITCH: *(she holds the stone high, all her attention on it)* I bid you
           goodbye, little Hebrew breaker of spells.

Cymbal.

NARRATOR: Israel threw the water in the jug over the witch, but some
           splashed the demon too, and as the witch disappeared,
           whirling around with a fearful cry and dragging the demon
           with her, all that remained was a small fish panting on the
           ground.

Israel kneels on the ground and scoops up the "fish" into the jug.

ISRAEL: *(slips his hand into the jug)* Swim, demon fish, swim for
           all time. Now I will place the jug *here* and only the birds
           and I will ever know where you are.

The jug is returned to its original place.

NARRATOR: And Israel and the village where he lived was without evil
           for many years.

Bells sound.

Activities to Use with
The Enchanted Spring

Additional information and vocabulary

TORAH (Hebrew): The Bible, specifically the first five books of Moses. The book of law.

TALMUD (Hebrew): Contains explanations and interpretation of ancient laws as well as answers to problems faced in daily life.

SYNAGOGUE: The house of prayer, but also a place to study and a community meeting place. The Rabbi leads the congregation in prayer here.

THE EVIL EYE: Many ethnic groups speak of the evil eye. In the past it was often believed that evil forces are particularly dangerous to the intelligent and gifted, or a good-looking child.

UNCLEAN: It was believed that certain animals, such as the pig, were particularly unclean, but the blood of any animal that has died and not been slain in the ritual way outlined by kosher law would fall under this category.

YOM KIPPUR, ALSO CALLED THE DAY OF ATONEMENT: The most holy of Jewish observance days, a day of fasting and prayer, when the congregation asks for forgiveness of any sins committed in the past year. The naming of the dead is observed. The *Torah* scrolls, which are kept in the Ark, or special cupboard, are read as part of the service.

In ancient times it was believed that crop failures, drought, and other natural disasters were a punishment for wrongdoing.

Discussion

From the reading of the play and the stage directions, what information can be obtained about the Jewish religion in the 19th century?

In what way is Israel typical of the usual hero/heroine of folktale and legend?

Throughout the ages, in times of trouble and persecution, people have told and written stories and plays, thinly disguising real problems they have had. Is *The Enchanted Spring* a parable? What reasons for or against this interpretation can be found in the play?

A warm-up game: Demon's touch

The demon's touch can instantly turn anyone to stone. One person is chosen to play the demon, while the rest of the class are villagers. A time limit is imposed, say thirty seconds. The demon must "freeze" as many villagers as possible. Repeat, this time in slow motion. Anyone who speeds up is disqualified in this round.

Acting, improvisation, and text

1. Character motive

When the witch knocks on the door and confronts Israel's mother, she uses very few words to announce who she is, why she is there, and what she intends to do. Students can work on similar scenes in twos or threes. There should be no prior discussion. The visitor, who must be unwelcome for some reason, is restricted to about six lines to make clear the purpose of the visit, and who he or she is. Included could be a ten-second silence when the characters see each other for the first time. Each student has a turn at being the visitor. This is an interesting exercise to share with the class. Time is required for each student to prepare the purpose of the visit.

2. Scenes of listening and response

Students may work on the following situations in pairs or small groups and reverse roles each time:

(a) listening to instructions, and following them exactly or not.
(b) hearing a threat, or bad news about oneself or someone else.
(c) listening as intentional eavesdropping, or overhearing something by accident.

Each scene should be complete, showing who is involved and in what way, and what happens as a result of the listening. What is the motive on both sides, and how is the scene resolved?

The next step is to identify the various kinds of listening in the text of the play, and work on them.

3. Warning

Students improvise a scene of warning, both given and received. If this warning is passed on to a third person, is there a change in interpretation from, say, teacher to mother to child, or friend to friend to friend? For example:

Teacher: "Tracy is not working hard enough."

Mother: "Your teacher said you'll fail your grade if you don't do better."

4. Scene titles

The title of each scene indicates its content: 1) "The drought"; 2) "The witch and the demon"; 3) "The knock on the door"; 4. "Unclean"; 5. Turn him to stone"; 6) "Evil overcome".

How do we shape titles and scenes?

In groups of four:

(a) Students each take a scene and talk through it in their own words, making sure that the plot line is clear.

(b) Each scene title is represented in movement. When the group is satisfied with the image, it is frozen.

(c) Each title can be used as the basis for a totally new improvised scene. This method is particularly useful in a rehearsal period which has lost some of its sparkle, and will bring the cast back to the text with renewed energy.

5. Flashback

In the play the narrator is telling the audience about a boyhood memory which is then acted out; from time to time the narrator reminds the audience of this, and also moves the story along. In groups of four or five, students take turns to tell about incidents in their lives. One incident is chosen by each group to dramatize. The person whose memory it is is both the playwright and the director. The scene should be worked on until the group is ready to perform it.

Voice and sound

The witch is described as "hissing" her words. Students should experiment with different voices for the birds, the demon, and the witch. When the birds speak they are accompanied by a "magical" sound of bells, or perhaps a flute, or any kind of sound the company wants to create. Musical sounds might also be effective for the witch and the demon. Groups could try different ways of enriching the text in this way.

The Magic Sieve

Cast

NARRATOR *Male / Female*
SISTER *Female*
BROTHER *Male*
HIS WIFE *Female*
FISHERWOMAN *Female*
GOBLIN 1 *Male / Female*
GOBLIN 2 *Male / Female*
GOBLIN 3 *Male / Female*
GOBLIN 4 *Male / Female*
GOBLIN 5 *Male / Female*
NEIGHBORS 1 to 5 *(may be double-cast as the goblins) Male / Female*
SPIRIT OF THE SIEVE *Male / Female*

Staging

The boat may be represented by an upturned bench or a riser, and may remain on stage throughout.

A pair of bamboo screens set upstage are useful for entrances and exits, and are sufficient to suggest various locations.

Props

Charcoal brazier (a low waste-paper basket), one for each family.
Jewelry.
A large sieve.
A log of wood.
A corncake or muffin.
A fishing net or rope.
A tatami or woven mat.
A small bowl.
A white sheet or cloth.
A fan (optional). In Kabuki theatre, the folding fan is considered a very important prop because of its flexibility: held open, half-shut, or closed, it represents a variety of moods and objects. When closed, it can become a knife, a pen, or any long, thin object.

The goblins may be played by actors holding small stick masks. In one recent production, the students cut out face shapes from felt pieces, gave each a "goblin-like appearance", then stiffened the faces by backing them on to pieces of cardboard, and stapling the whole to the front of twelve-inch pieces of dowel.

Costumes

Simple clothes. If available, short kimonos.
The Spirit of the Sieve should wear something white.
The Fisherwoman (who, in some productions, may be double-cast as the Spirit of the Sieve) needs a large, shabby shawl.

The Magic Sieve
Based on a Japanese folktale

When the play opens the two families are already on stage, side by side, separated by an imaginary thin wall between their houses. The characters are frozen, until each one begins to speak. The wealth of the sister may be suggested by her dress and jewels.

NARRATOR: Two relatives, whose fortunes had separated, prepared to welcome in the New Year.

BROTHER: The brother. . .

WIFE: His wife. . .

SISTER: And his sister. . .

NARRATOR: Lived next door to each other.

SISTER: The sister was very rich and had many things.

Sister puts on necklace and rings.

BROTHER: But her brother was poor; he did not even have enough coal left in his hibachi to heat his home.

The sister warms herself at her fire. The couple shivers.

WIFE: His wife longed to make rice cakes to celebrate the New Year, but alas, she had no rice. She asked her husband, "Please take this empty bowl and ask your sister, as a special favor, to lend us some rice."

Freeze.

BROTHER: So the brother went next door *(he bows)*. "We have no rice for New Year's breakfast. Will you lend us just a little? I will return it as soon as I can."

SISTER: I have none to spare *(turns him away)*.

He exits from the sister's house. Depending on staging, sister and wife should exit during next speech, removing any props with them.

BROTHER: The brother was ashamed to return home to his wife empty-handed. He decided to walk for a while. He took the path towards the sea. The day was as cold as his sister's words.

FISHERWOMAN: A fisherwoman was mending her nets. Her fingers were old and clumsy. She said, "Please, young man, help me turn my net."

BROTHER: Gladly.

FISHERWOMAN: Thank you, the net is heavy for my fingers. You are kind. Tell me, why do you look so sad? Don't you know that tomorrow is the Near Year?

BROTHER: Yes, but my wife and I go hungry, while others celebrate. The world is a cold and selfish place.

FISHERWOMAN: Not all the world is bad. You helped me; now I will help you in return. Take this corncake and go back along the path until you reach the mountains. Wait quietly, and you will see the mountain men. They will beg you for that cake. You may give it to them *only* in exchange for their sieve. Don't forget.

She exits.

BROTHER: The young man bowed his thanks and began to walk towards the mountains.

Goblins appear.

NARRATOR: A noise like a swarm of bees around a hive filled the air.

BROTHER: Those must be the mountain men the fisherwoman told me about. How noisy they are! I did not know they were goblins. They seem to be quarreling. I'll wait here and watch.

Goblins shout and push each other, trying to lift a log from a hole in the ground. They turn and see the brother and begin to drag him to the hole.

GOBLIN 1: A goblin was trapped there, and cried, "Help, murder, I'm caught under this log!"

BROTHER: The young man quickly freed him. "There you are," he said.

GOBLIN 1: The goblin did not bother to thank him. "I must have that corncake in your pocket; it smells better than all the things I have ever eaten."

BROTHER: The young man remembered what he had been told and said, "No, I cannot part with it."

NARRATOR: All the other goblins came 'round and offered him bribes for the cake.

GOBLIN 2: Give us the cake for our dinner and you shall have a bag of gold.

GOBLINS: Gold, gold, gold.

BROTHER: But the man would not change his mind. "I'll not exchange this cake for all the gold on the mountain."

NARRATOR: The goblins whispered together, greedily.

GOBLIN 3: "Not for all our mountain gold?" asked one.

GOBLIN 4: "That must be a very special cake," said another.

GOBLIN 5:   "What *will* you take for it?" pleaded the last.

BROTHER: The man looked around, pretending to consider for a long time, then he spoke: "I'll give you this special corncake for. . ."

GOBLINS: Yes, yes, go on, for what?

BROTHER: In exchange for the sieve in which you shake the mountain earth.

NARRATOR: The goblins put their heads together and argued loudly, but at last they said:

GOBLINS: We are all agreed.

The brother holds out the cake temptingly, just out of the goblins' reach. One of them holds out the sieve.

GOBLIN 1:   Here is our magic sieve. It cannot give you gold, but it will give you anything else that you really need. Treat it well.

GOBLIN 2:   When you make a wish you must turn the sieve to the right. . .

GOBLIN 5:   And when you have enough, then. . .

GOBLIN 3:   Turn the sieve to the left.

GOBLIN 4:   And don't forget to say, "Stop, sieve, stop."

GOBLIN 1:   Here.

Grabs the cake and runs, with other goblins.

NARRATOR: And all the goblins ran with it into the mountains, and were never seen again.

BROTHER: Holding the precious sieve the brother went home.

WIFE: His wife had been waiting anxiously for his return, for it was getting dark and cold. "Where have you been for so long? It is almost New Year. I hope you have brought the rice."

BROTHER: I have brought you something much better than a bowl of rice. Here is a magic sieve that will give us whatever we really need. Let's try it right away.

NARRATOR: They spread a clean tatami mat and put the sieve on it.

WIFE: Sieve, sieve, please make us some rice.

BROTHER: And he turned it to the right.

WIFE: The wife was amazed to see so much rice appear, enough for many meals.

BROTHER: Then her husband turned the sieve to the left, and said, "Stop, sieve, stop."

WIFE: This is a wonderful magic sieve. Let's share our good fortune and make a New Year's feast for all our friends and neighbors. And of course, we'll invite your sister too."

NARRATOR: All their neighbors and friends came and enjoyed the feast.

NEIGHBOR 1: What excellent food, such tasty fish and chicken!

NEIGHBOR 2: How kind of you to share your good fortune!

NEIGHBOR 3: You must have worked hard to provide all this for us.

NEIGHBOR 4: A feast to remember.

NEIGHBOR 5: May fortune be with you all through the years.

WIFE: Indeed.

BROTHER: The brother said, "It is nothing at all. There is plenty more
            for all of you, as much as you can eat."

SISTER: The sister looked on and was so full of envy that she could
            not eat. How could her brother afford all this, and where
            did it come from?
                She asked her brother, "Did you have a big catch yester-
            day after all?"

BROTHER: An old fisherwoman showed me a lucky place. Thank you
            for honoring us with your presence.

The neighbors bow and leave, followed by the sister, looking doubtful.

SISTER: This time she had to turn away, but she determined to dis-
            cover her brother's secret. That night, when all was quiet,
            she waited outside in the darkness and looked and listened.

She holds an open fan — the "wall" at which she listens.

WIFE: The wife put the sieve in a safe place and said, "Thank
            you for your magic gifts." And then she went to sleep.

The couple exits or sleeps.

SISTER: The sister crept into the house and stole the sieve. She
            walked down to the sea and climbed into a boat that she
            kept there. She rowed out to sea so that she could not be
            seen or heard. "I'll wish for gold," she said, and started
            to shake the sieve as hard as she could. "Make gold for
            me, lots of gold. . ."

The spirit of the sieve appears upstage.

SPIRIT OF THE SIEVE: Those who wish gold from me
            will get white salt to fill the sea.

NARRATOR: Then the sieve started to make salt.

SISTER: Who spoke? I have been tricked. I want gold, not salt! Help
           me, the salt is too heavy for the boat. It will sink! Stop,
           help me!

SIEVE: But the sieve went on pouring salt, and soon the boat was
           covered in white salt. Slowly the boat and the selfish sister
           and the magic sieve sank to the bottom of the sea.

*The spirit and the sister sink in slow motion to the ground, covered by a
white cloth that the spirit places over them. Freeze.*

NARRATOR: The sieve is still making salt, and that is why the sea will
           always taste salty.

Activities to Use with
The Magic Sieve

Discussion

1. This is a "Why?" play. Many cultures use "story" to explain why certain things happen. Students may already be familiar with a number of these tales, but they should be asked to find at least one other, preferably from their own ethnic roots, and be prepared to tell it for the rest of the class.
2. Several of the plays touch on relationships within the family unit. In *The Magic Sieve*, the sister is jealous of her brother, in spite of her own comfortable lifestyle. What explanation might there be for this sibling rivalry?
3. *The text says, "The man was ashamed to return empty-handed" after he had tried to borrow a little food from his sister.* In a later play, *Sungold*, a young wife is ashamed of her poor background and does not want her husband to see her shabby home. A discussion might revolve around different kinds of shame and embarrassment, and initiate further exchanges on similar or different kinds of feelings on the part of students.
4. The class decides, in the role of directors, on the number of scenes that are contained within the play. Each scene can be given a title, which would emphasize the core of the unit. For instance, one might be entitled "The Theft."

Warm-ups

1. Each student makes up the ideal menu for a New Year's party.
2. "I went to a multicultural party and I brought. . . ." Played along the lines of "I packed my bag." Each student repeats all the previous contributions and adds another one, and so on around the circle.
3. Tongue-twisters are a normal part of vocal warm-ups, and most classes have their own favorites. Sometimes a phrase or sentence in a play is hard to articulate clearly — e.g., in this play, "Slowly the boat and the selfish sister. . ." Students may compile their own favorite "difficult sentences" and work on them for speech practice. Partners exchange their "worst" three and listen to each other, at various distances from each other.
4. A variant of the wishing game. Students sit in one large circle, and a sieve or some fair-sized, round object is passed around. In turn, each stu-

dent must make a wish, turn the sieve to the right, turn the sieve to the left and say, "Stop, sieve, stop."

This should be performed as quickly as possible, and with very clear articulation. It's surprising how easily one can get mixed up, and it's a lot of fun.

5. Students get into groups of eight to twelve. They form a circle by linking hands.

(a) One student is inside the circle and pleads to be allowed out, meanwhile trying to find a weak link to do so; the circle attempts to prevent this in words and through maintaining linked hands.

(b) This time the student is outside the circle and must try to break in. Again the continuous improvised speech along the lines of "Let me in, I want to be with you" and the denial vocally and physically on the part of the group is important. Each student has a very short turn.

This game has many dramatic and social implications:

i) It is a good physical and vocal warm-up.

ii) It may be used with reference to any text where there is a real or symbolic struggle of any kind. For example, *The Magic Sieve* involves the struggle between the goblins and the brother, and the struggle for life by the sister and the salt that sinks her boat.

iii) The game may serve as preparation for an improvisation — e.g., wanting to join the "in-crowd", or trying to leave a gang.

Individual work: acting and improvisation

1. Students focus on the stealing of the sieve. In movement only, each in their own space, they interpret the act of listening to the conversation through the wall, looking through a crack to find out where the sieve is hidden, the decision to steal, the entry into the house in darkness, past the sleeping couple, and running off with the prized object.

2. The activity is repeated, but this time the character's thoughts are spoken aloud during the whole sequence.

3. Students decide whether to assume the role of the brother or his wife. Then, in a monologue, the brother expresses his feelings on being refused help by his sister, and how he feels about telling his wife. The wife expresses her thoughts (which will no doubt go through some changes) from the moment the husband leaves to borrow the rice through to the long wait for his return.

These activities will lend depth to the textual work, making the characters more real. In a multicultural situation it may often be difficult to ask for help and risk the fear of being refused. Scenes of asking, turning down, and giving help should be improvised, in order to experience every point of view, and to find solutions to difficult situations.

Pair work: the drowning

Pairs of students are asked to explore and experiment, in different styles, the moment from the sister's climb into the boat, to rowing out to sea, using the sieve incorrectly, and drowning by salt.

Each student should have the opportunity to play both the role of the sister and of the Spirit of the Sieve.

Each pair of students may then share their favorite moment with the class.

Group work: simultaneous work-through of the play

The class is divided into seven groups, each one including a narrator and made up of the number of students required for each scene. Thirty-one students can work simultaneously in this way. Each group must be given sufficient time to discuss character and motivation in the scene they are working on. All work is in improvised dialogue at this stage.

GROUP 1. Works on the relationship between the two families, and includes a scene *before* the play begins that clarifies the feelings between the brother, the sister, and the wife. Cast of four (including narrator).

GROUP 2. Explores the scene between the brother and the fisherwoman. Is the fisherwoman other than she seems to be? Groups may elaborate on any textual theories or ideas to strengthen the work. Cast of three (including narrator).

GROUP 3. Works on the meeting with the goblins. There should be a clear idea of what has happened just prior to the brother's arrival, and of the nature of the goblins' work. Students elaborate on the creation of different types of mountain men, each with a distinctive voice, walk, and attitude; and the verbal and physical exchange between the goblins and the brother. Cast of seven (including narrator).

GROUP 4. Works on the arrival of the brother, the trying out of the gift, and the decision to have a big New Year's celebration for the whole neighborhood. Cast of three (including narrator).

GROUP 5. Stages the actual celebration. The students make decisions about the neighbors and their relationship to the brother and his wife. They must know of their poverty. What kind of conversation at the party is not heard by the host? What is the sister's public behavior, and how does she conceal her real feelings? The scene ends with the hiding of the sieve. Cast of nine (including narrator).

GROUP 6. Begins as the party is over, and the sister determines to steal the treasured object. Cast of two — the sister and the narrator.

GROUP 7. This is the final scene, ending in the death of the sister and the loss of the sieve. Cast of three (including narrator).

Initially the entire class (groups can be amalgamated if the class size is smaller than thirty) works simultaneously, exploring and discussing their scenes, and trying out different possibilities. After thirty or forty minutes, the play can be run through in chronological order, each group sharing their scenes with the rest of the class.

Many of the ideas discovered will probably be retained in the final production when students return to the words of the text.

Work on space

Groups are given a word or phrase on a piece of paper — e.g., a hole in the ground, a mountain, a cave.

They have five minutes to present a very short scene with dialogue that will make clear to the audience what the designated space is. The actual word must not be mentioned. For example, a group of people looking down a "well" and discussing what or who is down there would, by the nature of the grouping and positioning of the bodies, make the word quite apparent.

Extended improvisation: future scenes

The sieve is no longer in its hiding place. Who discovers the theft? How many days is it since it was put away? What is it wanted for? Who is suspect? Students create a new scene about the mystery.

The Blind Hunter

Cast

NARRATOR / MUSICIAN *Male / Female*
HUNTER *Male / Female*
MOTHER *Female*
LOON *Male / Female*
BEAR *(optional) Male / Female*

Staging

This play is particularly effective outdoors.

When presented inside, any lighting effects enhance the drama. This may be as basic as switching off one of the classroom lights, or covering a couple of flashlights with blue paint or gel.

A simple sheet as a backdrop, and lights placed on the floor at each side, will cast shadows on the actors. A light placed *behind* the sheet between actors manipulating puppets, or acting themselves as spirits, is simple and looks very dramatic.

The igloo may be suggested in various ways — a sketch on a white backdrop, or a half-circle flat on the ground marked with masking tape, will encourage movement in a prescribed shape; a half-circle standing upright like a rainbow shape, made from white cardboard, could also be evocative. A sense of space and confinement is all that is required. The "bear" can be shot facing upstage, and need never be seen, unless the production requires a masked actor as a symbol.

Costumes

Winter parkas with hoods for the Inuit.
A bird mask for the loon.
Bear mask (optional).

Props

A bow and arrow. This is easily made by finding a natural piece of wood and fastening a piece of twine or string to its ends.
A simulated oil lamp, something looking like a deep pie dish, easily made from papier mâché.

An ulu (knife carried by Inuit women).
A "bear skin" (an off-white hearth rug or even a piece of shag carpeting).

Sound effects

Drumming and vocal sounds.
Guidance to a possible look for the staging will be found in the bright-colored pictures and pencil sketches of *Pitseolak: Pictures out of My Life*, by Pitseolak (Oxford University Press, 1978).

This play has been performed in the classroom and on stage by drama students. Some worked with only their own movements and acting and the various levels found in their drama rooms, others used a basic set design, props, and lights. Both sorts of productions were equally effective.

The Blind Hunter
Based on a legend of the Inuit

The setting is the Arctic, inside and outside an igloo.

The sounds of the Arctic begin the play: an Arctic loon calling, the wind moaning. The hunter and his mother sit motionless beside a stone lamp.

NARRATOR: When I was a boy, my father would tell me all the old stories of animals, of the spirits, of good and bad shamans.

As the narrator begins the story, the mother and the young hunter come to life in their places at the kudlik (seal-oil lamp).

NARRATOR: There was a young hunter and his mother, who lived on the edge of our settlement a long time ago. They say she was not one of the settlement, her ways were strange, she came from elsewhere. Her son was a good hunter: seal, fox, and ptarmigan returned to his spear, and he had already killed his first bear.

Hunter mimes stalking the animals, spearing a seal through a hole in the ice, cutting up meat with his knife, and piling more and more animals on the platforms around the igloo.

MOTHER: The mother cleaned and scraped, and dried and cooked, and there was no rest for her from sewing and mending.

The hunter brings her his parka to patch.

HUNTER: I am tired from the day's hunt, I will sleep now.

MOTHER: She had no rest and she began to hate him, and so she made a magic song. . .

She waits until her son is asleep and then begins her preparations.

And mixed up the brains of the Arctic fox, and of a hunter sealed in ice, with whale blubber, and smeared her son's sleeping eyelids with the ointment.

When she has finished pounding the mixture, she speaks softly:

Seal the light,
Close off his sight,
Blind, blind, blind.

She returns to her place at the lamp. The hunter wakes up and slowly discovers that he cannot see. The mother watches him.

HUNTER: What spirit did I offend yesterday? Whom must I now appease? Mother, you will have to bring me food now, for I am blind and helpless.

MOTHER: "What there is, you will share." And she threw him only scraps, but she ate well.

NARRATOR: It was a long winter, and the woman had rest and time enough, and plenty to eat. The hunter had provided well for them. But she lied to him:

MOTHER: The food is almost gone.

NARRATOR: One day a polar bear stood outside the ice window of the igloo, and tried to get in.

Bear (optional) stands outside.

HUNTER: Mother, I hear the bear's hot breath, and smell his wet fur. Bring me my bow and guide my arm, so that I may shoot to kill.

The mother stands beside him and guides his arm. He shoots, there is the sound of a great weight falling.

HUNTER: Mother, I heard the ground tremble, the bear fell. Now we will have fresh meat at last.

He tries to move to the igloo opening, but she pushes him aside.

MOTHER: "You missed him, poor blind creature. Sit in your corner."
            And she did not share the meat with him.

NARRATOR: And so the winter drew on, and the hunter grew weaker.

A loon cries. The hunter hears it and crawls to the door of the igloo.

HUNTER: I can smell the warm air; the voice of the loon tells me that
            winter has passed. Ice break-up. The world I cannot see
            is beautiful. I will get to the water.

*Slowly he makes his way to the water's edge. His mother is nowhere in sight.
A loon appears.*

LOON: I can help you find your sight. We will dive under the water
            and wash away the bad magic.

HUNTER: You are a powerful helper, but how can you carry me on
            your small wings, even though I am weak after the long
            winter, and how will I not choke in the icy water?

LOON: You must trust me! Climb on my back and hold on to my
            neck.

NARRATOR: Then the hunter put his arms around the loon's neck and
            the loon, whose spirit strength could make him lift kayaks,
            dove under the water and rose again.

LOON: What do you see?

HUNTER: I see light, bright and white as ice.

LOON: Then your eyes do not see enough.

NARRATOR: A second time the loon and the boy dove beneath the water
            and came back up for air.

LOON: What do you see now?

HUNTER: I see the whole world and all that is in it.

LOON: Then you see too much.

NARRATOR: One more time they disappeared under the water, and this time when they returned to land, the hunter said:

HUNTER: I see as I did before, and I fear I will die of joy and of cold!

LOON: You will not die, and you will live to be a great hunter, and they will sing songs for you and me, the loon and the boy who was blind.

NARRATOR: And the loon flew off, calling the coming of spring.

The hunter returns home, where his mother is scraping a skin with her ulu.

HUNTER: Tell me, Mother, is that the skin from the bear that I killed when I was blind?

MOTHER: "No, my son," said his mother, "it was left for pity for me by a passing hunter."

NARRATOR: They looked into each other's eyes, and each knew the truth.

HUNTER: I need to become strong again. Come with me to catch whale; the ice is breaking.

MOTHER: The woman dared not refuse, now that she knew her son could see.

NARRATOR: They walked to the shore and climbed into their kayak, and the hunter threw his harpoon into the fat side of a whale, and tied the other end of the line around his mother's arm.

HUNTER: Help me drag in the whale!

NARRATOR: But the whale began to drag and twist to free himself from the harpoon, and the mother called to her son.

MOTHER: Help me, my son.

HUNTER: I cannot help you, Mother. *(looks away)*

NARRATOR: The whale dragged the woman into the water and under the waves. Her cries became one with the whale, and she was never seen again. They say that she became a Narwhale. If you listen to the voices of the whales you can hear the cry of the woman dragged forever through the water for her wickedness.

The play ends with the loon flying around the hunter and the kayak. There is a moment of stillness, and then the cry of the whales is heard again.

Activities to Use with
The Blind Hunter

Background material

An excellent source for information, paintings, drawings, and interviews may be found in *Pitseolak: Pictures out of My Life* (Oxford University Press, 1978) and *Uumajut, Animal Imagery in Inuit Art* (Winnipeg Art Gallery, 1985).

These books can help students to understand the significance of the Spirit World in Inuit life, and the importance of animals in this spiritual culture. The loon is a strong spirit, often a helper of the Shaman (Angakok), a go-between, or interpreter, between the natural and the spiritual worlds. The loon is a guardian of those who use the kayak, and its ability to disappear under the water and reappear unharmed, as well as its distinctive, haunting cry, make it as respected as any other Arctic animal.

The bear is both the fiercest and the strongest opponent of man, and at the same time a powerful spirit helper.

As in many other cultures, a wrongdoing by a member of the community may result in some kind of retribution by the spirit world. One of the best known of the "retribution" legends is that of Sedna, the goddess of the sea, who prevents animals from being caught, thus starving the people who have offended her. She was, according to the legend, originally an orphan girl, who was ill treated (very uncharacteristically, and contrary to all tribal laws) and she was then transformed, after being cast off, and from that time ruled the underwater kingdom.

Mood, movement, and text

1. After the play has been read and discussed, students contribute a word or phrase they remember from the text — e.g., dark, cold, blind, death. The teacher or group leader repeats each word, which is then interpreted in movement by the students in their own space. All work simultaneously, but may later share their work.

2. Students are asked to move in different ways and imagine different surfaces and climatic conditions — e.g., hunting an animal at different times of day, for sport or for food. Students must decide before each movement *where* they are, at *what* time of day, and *why* they are moving in a particu-

lar way. Examples may be taken from within as well as outside the text. Students should work individually, but at the same time.

3. In small groups, students talk through the play, making sure that they are secure about the sequence of events. Then the whole play is worked through in movement only.

The play lends itself well to this kind of approach, and the tensions, conflicts, and narrative should become very clear.

Improvisation and acting

1. Groups make up "headings" for different parts of the play. These become improvisation. Appropriate scene titles might include: "The hunt" (and how a hunt might be reversed), "Magic potion", "Blindness", "Deceit".

2. Individually, students working in their own spaces explore the idea of waking up one morning to find that they have been deprived of one of their senses. There may be discussion and sharing of some of their feelings before returning to the text. Students could contrast loss, as well as partial or complete restoration, of the sense, as in *The Blind Hunter: The Miracle Worker* by William Gibson, about Helen Keller. The book contains useful scenes for further work on the senses.

3. In groups, students set up a working "stage" space, including props and furniture to make the area distinct. Then work begins on familiarizing themselves with the set. When this is done, students attempt to move smoothly around the space blindfolded: they try to find a particular object, move to a door or entrance, etc. In order to act "blind", it is important for students to become familiar with the handicap in this way. Small groups may work simultaneously in different areas of the drama room.

4. Students work in pairs on the problem of carrying someone. They might discuss under what circumstances this would occur, and then build a short scene in which this happens. A friend has an accident; a small child cannot cross a stream; etc. Then work continues on the carrying of the boy by the loon.

Transformation

Students are given time to look at pictures of Inuit art and sculpture, and then each in their own space is asked to transform slowly into the image they have chosen. After a while, vocal sounds and movement should be encouraged. Students then share their work with the class, with positive discussion being led by the teacher.

Voice

Making projecting the voice part of the play sometimes works better than continual reminders to speak up.

Divide the class into four groups. Group A consists of hunters lost in the blizzard. Group B makes the sounds of storm. Group C calls out trying to locate the hunters, and giving its own position. Group D is the audience and listens critically. After thirty seconds, the "blizzard" is stopped and everyone is given feedback on audibility. Groups rotate. Ideally, voice work is done outdoors, or in a gym. This is a very noisy exercise! It is also important for the teacher to set the mood by vividly sketching the environment and demanding concentration and belief in the situation — i.e., trying to make oneself heard under very difficult conditions.

Questions to ask after group presentation of the text

It is always interesting for the whole class to work on each play simultaneously and in groups, and then to watch others' efforts. The feedback for each group should emphasize that there are many ways of presenting a play, and different approaches may give many unique ideas for a final concept.

Sample questions:
How did the groups use contrast in voice and movement?
Were the group members able to sustain their concentration?
Was the hunter able to put across his longing, fear, shame, and loss?
Did the groups use the space to show the distance travelled?
If so, how did they do this?
What new ideas did the groups introduce?
Did the groups manage to sustain the atmosphere of ice and cold?

Narration

One of the first problems the cast may encounter is the relationship between narrator and actor; a decision will have to be made as to whether the action follows immediately after the narration or happens simultaneously, or whether the actors initiate the action. All kinds of storytelling activities will already have been experienced in drama or language arts class. A good revision might involve, as follows:

1. In groups of four or five, rehearse and tell a simple story that is familiar, then hand over the narration to different group members, keeping the flow of the story. Every part of the story must be acted out while the story is being told.

2. In the Inuit dance house (the community igloo) where stories used to be told, whole portions of the narrative — ice, animals, even the wind — would be acted out by the storyteller. Students can work on individual narrations of portions of the text and act out each part of the story. The result is a very lively solo presentation.

Sungold

Cast

NARRATOR *Male / Female*
MOTHER *Female*
DAUGHTER *Female*
BEGGERWOMAN *Female*
PRINCE *Male*
SERVANTS FOR SCENE CHANGES/SUN
(optional) Male / Female

Staging

The play contains a number of journeys, so arena or horseshoe staging works particularly well. The narrator continues to speak from his or her place close to the audience (the narrator is, of course, free to move from place to place also) while characters travel either behind the audience or around the acting space.

The Pîpal tree can be a cut-out, or be represented by a riser, tall stool, or step-ladder.

The hut needs nothing other than a low table and simple sleeping mat. Brightly colored floor cushions will transform this into the palace. A simple screen upstage can be used for exits and entrances, and a bright cloth can be thrown over it to indicate the palace.

Lighting

Light is the easiest way to indicate the "sun". There are several other possible ideas: a large "sun" banner held by two actors; a huge, gold-colored paper circle, or even a fan-shaped circle, makes an effective symbol; a large papier-mâché sun mask raised on a stick.

Costumes

Ideally, costumes should reflect the Punjabi style of dress. Both mother and daughter are barefoot when poor, but wear jewelry and sandals when rich.

Props

A straw broom.

A cup (possibly made to look as though made of leaves) called *Dôna*, and used by the very poor.

A gold-sprayed goblet.

Rings.

Bracelets.

Two chapatti (unleavened pancake bread).

A simple cotton square in which to wrap the chapatti.

A begging bowl.

A sun image (see "Lighting").

Additional information

Pîpal tree

A fig tree. Its big leaves are valued for shade. Sometimes the leaves are also used in divination. In folktale and legend, the Pîpal tree is said to be the refuge of liars, witches, and thieves.

Sungold
Based on a Punjabi folktale

NARRATOR: The sun shines into every corner of the great land that is called India. Long ago, a mother and daughter lived in great poverty. They had very little, enough for only one meal of bread a day. Their only gold was the light that shone through the cracks in the walls of their hut, and so they worshipped the sun.

MOTHER: Never forget that we must share all that we have, and give it gladly in the name of the sun.

DAUGHTER: I will honor the sun always.

The mother smiles and leaves for work.
Daughter sweeps the floor, then looks at two small loaves of bread hungrily.

NARRATOR: *(speaking while the daughter does the chores)* Sometimes it was very hard to live like that.

DAUGHTER: I am so hungry today; surely Mother won't mind if I eat my share before she returns from work.

She eats, then wraps her mother's loaf in a clean cotton square.
She sits on the stoop at the entrance of the hut.
A beggerwoman passes, then she stops.

BEGGARWOMAN: Good day, child, may I rest a while?

DAUGHTER: Gladly. You should not be walking in the heat of the day.

She gets her a cup of water.

Must you go far today?

The beggerwoman drinks.

BEGGARWOMAN: I travel the long roads of India as far as I can, summer and winter. An empty stomach is not a good traveling companion. *(she eyes the wrapped bread)* Could you spare a chapatti?

DAUGHTER: This is my mother's evening meal; I wish you had come sooner. I would have shared mine with you, but today I ate early.

BEGGARWOMAN: I *think* she would say, in honor of the sun who shines on us all, rich and poor alike: "Eat from my portion."

DAUGHTER: I don't know. She will be hungry after the long day's work.

BEGGARWOMAN: You are a good girl; you say you would share your bread, your mother taught you well. Come, listen to her words.

The daughter still hesitates, then hears in her mind her mother's voice:

VOICE OF MOTHER: Never forget we must give gladly.

Daughter breaks the loaf and gives the beggerwoman half.

DAUGHTER: Take it, and may the sun watch over you on your journey.

BEGGARWOMAN: I thank you in her name.

She exits.

NARRATOR: That night the mother returned a little later than usual. She was tired and hungry.

Mother enters. She sits down, and the daughter gives her the half-loaf.

MOTHER: Only half! Where is the rest?

DAUGHTER: A beggarwoman came by and asked for food. She said I should honor the sun as you had taught me. Don't be angry, Mother. I had already eaten my share, only yours was left.

MOTHER: You gave her my share and *then* you ate your own, greedy
             girl, so you begrudged a share of *your* food.

DAUGHTER: Believe me, Mother, all mine was already gone. Forgive
             me. I'm telling you the truth.

MOTHER: Easy to say, as easy as giving away what is not yours to give!

DAUGHTER: You shall have all my bread tomorrow. I'm sorry.

MOTHER: Tomorrow will not feed me now! I'll hear no more! Out
             of my sight — you dishonor the sun.

The mother goes to her sleeping corner and turns away from her daughter.

DAUGHTER: She is so angry with me, she doesn't want me here any
             longer. I don't know what to do. I'll leave.

The daughter goes out, taking nothing with her.

NARRATOR: She walked and walked, her eyes full of tears. It grew late,
             she did not know where she was, and she was afraid.

DAUGHTER: I'll stay here in the shade of this Pîpal tree. Oh, Sun, please
             help me, I do not want to walk the roads like a beggar.

She puts her head in hands and cries. A young man enters. He is a prince.

NARRATOR: A prince who had been out hunting wolves found the
             unhappy girl.

PRINCE: I know that the Pîpal tree shelters witches and liars and
             ghosts, but surely they would be hiding up in the tree, and
             not on the ground. I will ask her who she is. Are you lost?
             Do stop crying and tell me what you are doing alone so
             far from home.

DAUGHTER: I am lost and I shelter here because I am alone. I have no
             mother, no house, no home.

The prince helps her to her feet.

PRINCE: You need never be alone again. You are gentle and beautiful, and you shall be my wife. My palace is close by. Come with me.

They exit.

NARRATOR: And so the girl, who had known only poverty, lived the life of a rich princess, surrounded by servants and admiring and loving friends. She was grateful to the sun who had brought her such happiness, but she was afraid it could not last.

Daughter enters dressed as a princess.

DAUGHTER: The other women look at me strangely sometimes. They wonder where I come from, for I never speak of my mother or my home. How can I? If they knew the truth they would despise me and turn away from me. Oh, great sun, I don't want my mother to find me; I am sure she is out searching for me.

NARRATOR: One day a visitor arrived, dressed in rags.

Mother enters.

DAUGHTER: Mother, how did you find me? Please don't tell anyone who you are. You must leave at once.

MOTHER: I heard of your good fortune, and I have come to share it, as we once shared everything.

DAUGHTER: Of course I will. Here, take this ring, and my bracelets too, but then you must leave here.

MOTHER: Ungrateful girl, is this how you show honor to the sun? You owe all that you have to me. It was because I sent you to seek your way in the world that you have found a rich husband; and this is the thanks you give me.

DAUGHTER: Your words punished me so harshly once, I might have starved. But now, if you stay here, it will be an even greater punishment, for I will be humiliated and disgraced. *(ashamed)* My husband does not know who I am.

Daughter turns away.

OFFSTAGE VOICE OF PRINCE: Where is the princess, why is she not here to greet me?

DAUGHTER: Oh, sun, help me once more.

The mother exits silently. Where she stood, a gold goblet appears. The mother brought this in earlier, concealed under her clothes. Prince enters.

PRINCE: I thought I heard voices.

DAUGHTER: I was praying to the sun for our happiness to go on for always.

PRINCE: Nothing could ever come between us. *(he picks up the goblet)* Where did this fine goblet come from? I don't remember it.

DAUGHTER: It comes from my mother's house.

PRINCE: I long to see the place you came from. Let us prepare to go there right away.

Exit.

DAUGHTER: Oh, mighty sun, my life is a lie; I truly love my husband, please help me again.

Exit.

NARRATOR: And so they made the journey back to her old home. Before they reached the place, her mother came to welcome them, dressed in fine clothes.

The hut is ablaze in gold. Sun image is held up high, or there is a light transformation.

PRINCE: You did not tell me your home is a palace. It shimmers like gold.

The prince and the daughter and the mother remain still during the next speech, frozen in the moment of greeting.

NARRATOR: They stayed together peacefully for three days, and then set off for their own palace.

The freeze is broken, the mother exits, and the prince and his wife start their return journey.

NARRATOR: They had only gone a little way when the prince stopped.

DAUGHTER: Is something wrong? Why are we waiting? I am anxious to return before nightfall.

PRINCE: Why do you seem so eager to leave this gracious home behind? I want to look again at its golden roof.

The sun image is lowered or light fades.

DAUGHTER: *(she has a sense of impending disaster)* Surely you have seen enough of it these past three days. Let us go to our own palace.

Meanwhile the prince is searching the horizon and is puzzled.

PRINCE: Where your palace stood there is only a hovel, and a poor old woman sweeping the stoop.

DAUGHTER: You must be mistaken. Perhaps it is just a cloud of dust that makes it look like this.

PRINCE: The sky is clear. There is no dust. (*He looks at her and sees her distress. She knows she cannot maintain the deceit.*)

Now I know why you have seemed so strange these past days. You have cheated me. Go back to the tree where I found you, liar.

DAUGHTER: I deserve those words. Yes, I lied to you. I am a poor girl, born in that hut (*indicates hut*), and the woman is my mother. We have always worshipped the sun, and it was she who answered my prayers. And when I left home, she sent you to find me. I was ashamed of my poverty and so said nothing. I was wrong. I know that now.

Mother appears.

MOTHER: I have harmed us all and caused shame and misery.

PRINCE: I, too, was wrong. The past is over. (*to daughter*) You have brought me much happiness. Let us go now and sit a while in your house, and tell me all your story.

They exit.

NARRATOR: They lived peacefully for the rest of their lives and continued to love and honor the sun.

Activities to Use with *Sungold*

Discussion

1. Many of the characters in this book are either good or evil to an extreme degree. The mother and daughter, however, have many contradictory qualities, being sometimes honest and kind, and at other times mean or deceitful. Ask the students to give a verbal or written portrait of either character.

2. Although this story is hundreds of years old, and originated in that part of India now known as the Punjab, the incidents and emotions are universal.

Students, in small groups or as a class, identify these, and make comparisons with their own experiences. For example, their mother comes home from work and is tired and irritable, or she is a widow or divorcée and the only breadwinner. Life is not easy. The girl has mixed feelings of shame at her deceit for denying her family origins, and feels embarrassed when her mother appears dressed so humbly.

3. Students are asked to talk about the following statement: "a life based on a lie". In what way does this refer to the play?

4. Students are asked to find out how many different kinds of worship are practised in India and in Pakistan.

Warm-up activity

Students sit in a circle. Each one makes one statement about the power or beauty of the sun, as though she were the mother or daughter explaining her reasons for honoring the sun — e.g., "All light comes from the sun," and so on around the circle.

Acting and improvisation

1. Students in pairs are asked to read the scene between the beggar woman and the daughter. Then, similar situations from contemporary life are improvised. For instance, Susan has been allowed to borrow her sister's new bicycle for the afternoon. Her best friend, Amanda, tries to persuade Susan to lend the bicycle to her. Students are encouraged to experiment with different kinds of persuasion, bribes, threats, ingenuity, etc., before returning to the text.

2. Quarrels and accusations.

Pairs or threes explore:

(a) Domestic arguments of various kinds. In the play the daughter leaves home, a drastic solution to an argument. Actors drawing on their own experience of similar disputes find different ways to solve the quarrels.

(b) Arguments that have a basis in accusation. For instance, the daughter is accused by her mother of stealing, and by her husband of witchcraft. A modern argument might be, "You stole my diary and read it, and now everyone knows about me."

Students should make sure they take on the role of both the accused and the accuser.

(c) Apologies. The daughter apologizes to her mother, afraid of her anger. The prince apologizes to his wife because he loves her and doesn't want to lose her.

Some apologies are insincere, or are given for ulterior motives. Students should experiment with scenes of various kinds of apology.

3. "She heard of her daughter's good fortune, and decided she was entitled to share it."

Students may use this as the opening line of a play of their own devising. The style is story theatre. Students can refer back to *The Talking Fish* to remind themselves of an example of this style of play, where the character describes her own actions — e.g., "She smiled and went on her way" — as well as speaking the dialogue.

4. Missing scene. A play will often refer to an offstage incident, or ask the audience and the actors to accept that certain things have taken place. One such *implied* scene would be when the daughter arrives at the palace. She is admired greatly and becomes the focus of devoted friends and servants. Students may make up this "missing" scene. Ask them to think about kinds of questions the princess would have to answer, and what conversations might take place. How would the daughter conceal her background? Does she miss her mother among all these strangers? The scene could be scripted and later inserted in the play.

5. Leaving home. Leaving home is a basic theme in many plays and books. Characters leave home to solve problems, to escape unhappiness, to search for independence. Have students improvise their own plays based on this theme.

Narration

The beggarwoman might experience many different kinds of welcome in her travels across the land. Small groups of three to five tell about imaginary incidents and then select some as the basis for improvisation.

For information on major religions of India — Hinduism, Sikhism, Buddhism, Islam — see *Ten Religions of the East,* by Edward Rice (Four Winds Press, 1978) or *Religious Beliefs* by John Mayled (Wayland Publishers Ltd., 1987).

The Captive Moon

Cast

GRANDMOTHER *Female*
CHILD *Male / Female*
GRANDMOTHER AS A YOUNG GIRL *Female*
WISE WOMAN *Female*
VILLAGER 1 *Male / Female*
VILLAGER 2 *Male / Female*
VILLAGER 3 *Male*
VILLAGER 4 *Male*
WILL O' WISP 1 *Male / Female*
WILL O' WISP 2 *Male / Female*
WITCH 1 *Male / Female*
WITCH 2 *Male / Female*
BOGLE 1 *Male / Female*
BOGLE 2 *Male / Female*
Moon *Female*
TREE SPIRIT *(one or more) Male / Female*
CRAWLING THING 1 *Male / Female*
CRAWLING THING 2 *Male / Female*

The cast may be enlarged by adding to the number of night creatures, or may be reduced by double casting. The grandmother, the child, the young girl, and the wise woman could be played by male actors, becoming grandfather, child, young boy, and wise man.

Additional background information

A will o' wisp (also known as jack o' lantern) is believed to be a wandering soul who cannot find rest in either heaven or hell. It usually takes the form of a malignant, mischievous imp, who will deliberately try to get travelers lost, chasing victims through mud and brambles until they are totally confused. The traveler is often lured to fen and marshland, where he or she will drown in a pool.

A Bogle is a sort of goblin, a bad-tempered creature (neither man nor animal) whose tricks are mean-spirited. A Bogle appears in Joseph Jacobs's tale, "The Cauld Lad of Hilton".

Staging

As with the other plays in this book, students will be able to create the effects of light and dark, good and evil, through acting and with a minimal set. Boxes, risers, levels of any sort can be used to create rocks and shadows.

If no light other than overhead classroom light is available, a flashlight held by a student standing on a chair, and candles or small pen lights held by the will o'wisps would be effective.

Costumes

MOON: A long dark cloak and hood.
MOON CREATURES: Dark clothes that allow freedom of movement. Students will have their own strong ideas as to costume pieces which will make their characters distinctive.
GRANDMOTHER AS A YOUNG GIRL: An apron over a simple dress.
VILLAGE PEOPLE: Homespun, plain clothing.

Sets and props

A stool for the grandmother.
A bench, box, or small table for the wise woman.
Two coins.
A mirror.
A cast-iron pot and spoon.
A leather-bound book.
Two small flashlights or candles in holders.

Music

Suitable music for the appearance of the night creatures may be found in: *Daphnis and Chloe,* by Ravel; *Création du Monde,* by Papathanassiou; *Pictures at an Exhibition* and *Night on a Bare Mountain*, by Moussorgsky; *Till Eulenspiegel's Merry Pranks*, by Richard Strauss; and *Tam O'Shanter*, by Arnold.

The Captive Moon

*Based on a Scottish folktale retold by
Joseph Jacobs*

The setting is a village on the edge of a marsh. Spindly trees, roots, and sparse tufts of grass cover treacherous pools and bogs. It is a dangerous place to cross in the dark.

The grandmother and the child are seated at stage right, close to the audience. The play opens with the sound of winds across the marsh. An owl hoots once or twice. The child runs to a "window" up left.

GRANDMOTHER: (*stands, turns upstage*) Come away from the window now, it's a dark, windy night out there.

CHILD: It's not really dark; I can see little lights.

GRANDMOTHER: Jack o'lanterns, I reckon. *(half to herself)* They almost caught me once.

CHILD: Oh, Gran, you're just saying that to. . .Look! *(points to the new moon)*

GRANDMOTHER: You should know better than to point at the new moon.

CHILD: I've got my penny ready. (*The child turns around, turns over the coin in her hand, shuts her eyes tightly, and wishes.*)

GRANDMOTHER: I remember once:

She and the child freeze. A flashback. Music.

Night creatures of different shapes prowl, scream, wail, and whisper hideously as they move through the shadows, looking for a victim. A young girl appears wearing an apron. She is out of breath, running to keep up

*with two pinpoints of light. They are held by will o'wisps who lure the girl
in circles. The other panting creatures are just beyond touching distance.
The girl is about to step into a bubbling bog pool, where the echoing voices
have led her.*

WILL O'WISPS: Here, here, here,
　　　　　　This way, this way,
　　　　　　Follow me, me, me. . .

Music off.

*Suddenly, as the moon appears, the will o'wisps' lights and the spirits vanish.
The girl, whose foot is poised over the pool, withdraws it quickly and shivers
in disgust.*

YOUNG GIRL: That's a nasty boggy place. Lucky for me the moon's up.
　　　　　　A new moon, here's my penny; there, I've turned it. (*she
　　　　　　wishes silently*) I'll be home in no time at all, with the moon
　　　　　　lighting the path for me. I must have been running in
　　　　　　circles.

She exits. Freeze end of scene.

GRANDMOTHER: I remember how the new moon saved me that night
　　　　　　from a watery grave, and I wasn't the only one. Terrible
　　　　　　stories are told about the wild things on the moor. You
　　　　　　know, most people stayed indoors when the moon was
　　　　　　taking her rest.

CHILD: 　　　She rests only for a little while, doesn't she?

GRANDMOTHER: That's how it should be, and mostly it is; but there
　　　　　　was a long time, when the moon seemed gone forever, and
　　　　　　the Bogles and witches and creeping things got so
　　　　　　troublesome. . . .

Music. Brief appearance of the spirits upstage of the grandmother.

GRANDMOTHER: that people wouldn't go out after dark, even to visit
　　　　　　their neighbors, and the dogs never stopped barking, and
　　　　　　had to be tied up.

It was a sad time for us, it seemed the moon was as good as dead.

Exit spirits. Music off.

CHILD: What did you do?

GRANDMOTHER: Only one thing to do, and that was to go and see the wise woman.

Enter wise woman. On a table/bench are a book, a mirror, and a pot. She stirs the pot, throwing in herbs from time to time. She is not necessarily old.

VILLAGER 1: We need your help. Can you tell us why the moon. . .

WISE WOMAN: (*interrupts and keeps on stirring*) I know why you're here. I saw you coming, heard you talk.

The villagers whisper together.

VILLAGER 2: She knows.

VILLAGER 3: Will she help us, then?

VILLAGER 4: Quiet, she sees something.

WISE WOMAN: (*speaks, seeing something in the pot*) The Bogles and spirits that hide in the shade, who worship the darkness to practise their trade, have captured the moon, extinguished her light, and that's why the moor is in darkness all night.

VILLAGER 1: What do you mean, "captured"?

WISE WOMAN: Drowned, and no one knows where.

VILLAGER 3: Look in the mirror, maybe it'll tell us where.

WISE WOMAN: There's a mist over the glass now. I can't see.

VILLAGER 4:   Won't you try stirring the pot again? It's gruesome without the comfort of the moon.

*The wise woman throws in more herbs, stirs the pot three times slowly, and
speaks as though from a long way off. The villagers huddle together, not
because they are afraid of the wise woman, but in fear of what she might
tell them.*

WISE WOMAN: I see a journey: not today, not tomorrow, but many nights
ago. It's the moon in her long cloak and hood to cover
her shining light hair, come to see what goes on when she's
at rest.

*There is a flashback, as in the opening sequence of the grandmother as
a girl. The villagers are still. Music. The moon enters, hooded and cloaked,
hugging herself from the cold and night sounds. The various spirits shadow
her and become bolder, but the moon shakes her hood free. Her hair sym-
bolizes the light, and the creatures retreat with signs and sounds of horror.*

SPIRITS: (*wailing*) Light, moonlight, bright.

*The moon walks on, but suddenly stumbles over a root or stick that has
been deliberately put in her way. She falls to her knees, puts out her hands
to steady herself, and her hood falls forward. The tree spirit's hands, like
underwater weeds, grasp hers and she cannot move. The twisted, screeching
shapes of the spirit surround the imprisoned moon. They freeze during
the next dialogue. Music soft.*

WISE WOMAN: Dark, all dark.

VILLAGER 4: Where is she? What are they doing now?

WISE WOMAN: Quiet, let me listen.

The spirits circle around the kneeling moon, poking and pulling at her.

WITCH 1:   You'll be out of our sight. . .

WITCH 2:   With your pale golden light.

BOGLE 1:   We're tired of hiding away.

BOGLE 2:   Spoiler of spells, now you shall pay.

CRAWLING THING 1: (*twists around the moon*) Torment and smother
            and choke.

CRAWLING THING 2: Twist her up tight in her cloak.

TREE SPIRIT: Hold her hands
            with iron bands.

SPIRIT 1:   Poison or drown her in icy water.

SPIRIT 2:   What shall we do with her, now that we've caught her?

WILL O'WISPS: No time, no time. (*they point to the sky*)

The moon crouches, terrified, holding her hands tightly.

WISE WOMAN: The mirror's clearing. That means it's almost daylight,
            they'll have to go, but they'll be back next night to tor-
            ment her, and decide what they'll do with her. Perhaps
            get rid of her for good.

VILLAGER 1: Can you see any more?

WISE WOMAN: Now they're lifting her up and laying her down in the
            water. There's a big slab of stone to keep her under the
            water. And a will o'wisp on each side, like a flickering can-
            dle, to guard.

*During the wise woman's description, the creatures have performed these
actions and then retreated into the shadows. Music off.*

VILLAGER 3: What's to happen now?

WISE WOMAN: You must go find her.

VILLAGER 1: How can we find her in the dark and the bogs?

VILLAGER 4: Yes, and her covered with slimey green water?

The wise woman looks in her book.

WISE WOMAN: This is what you must do: Just before nightfall and before the horrors come back, go across the marsh.

VILLAGER 2: How can we find the blessed moon if she's drowned? (*others shush him*)

WISE WOMAN: (*reading*) Look for the lights like candles, for the stone like a coffin, and the tree with arms like a cross. Don't be afraid. Put a stone in your mouth and don't speak one word until you reach home in safety. Remember to carry a twig of hazel with you as a protection.

She exits.

GRANDMOTHER: I remember I watched from the window as they set off the next evening, the twigs held fast in their hands. They must have been so afraid.

Freeze. Flashback.

The villagers depart. Sounds are heard that might be those of spirits or birds or wind, or all three. Occasionally a hand reaches out, or a face looms out of the grass.

CHILD: What happened then?

GRANDMOTHER: My father told me, for he was one of them, that when they reached the place, the lights of the will o'wisps moved around and around them. In their heads — for remember they could not speak — they said the "Lord's Prayer" forward and backwards to ward off the evil spirits. Then they pulled at the stone and dragged it off the moon, and she rose up, and threw back her hood, and the light blinded them for a moment. Then she was gone, back up in the sky, bright as ever. And so they came safely home — in light shining like day.

Villagers freeze.

CHILD: And is it all true?

GRANDMOTHER: Go to the window, bow to the new moon. Would I
tell you stories? It's as true as the light shining through
the window. (*she turns her coin*) And now, I'll make my
wish.

Activities to Use with
The Captive Moon

Discussion

1. The text refers to several superstitions about the moon. Students should identify these, then share others that they know about or practise themselves. For instance, it is considered good luck to wear an apron back to front when there's a new moon, and bad luck to look at the new moon through the branches of a tree.
2. The class may compile a list of names of supernatural creatures (both from the play and from elsewhere). To these may be added word images and characteristics suggested by the names.
3. Let each student create a personal make-up, mask, or character design for *one* of the supernatural creatures.
4. Music is very much a part of this play. The musical suggestions are a starting point only; students will likely wish to introduce their own choices, and also experiment with percussion and vocal sounds, in addition to or instead of taped music.
5. The play's emphasis is on light and dark. Small groups may brainstorm their ideas on creating the maximum theatrical effect. They may then share their ideas of a lighting plot, and the precise moments in the play when lighting should change, with the class.

Narration

1. The play contains powerful images and objects — the hooded cloak, the cauldron, the magic mirror, hazel twigs, stones, and coins. Small groups may be given one or two objects (not necessarily those mentioned) and create a scene or dramatized story built around the object(s).

   In an extension of this exercise, students may bring an object from home, perhaps from another culture, and share its meaning. Some stories will lend themselves to dramatization.
2. The "moon" may tell the story of her plight to a group of listening "stars", who may question her about her adventures.
3. The "father" may give his account of the final rescue to a group of four to seven, after he returns to his waiting and anxious family. The group should agree, prior to the story, who the members of the family are, and their attitudes to the expedition. Is the father brave, frightened, inclined to exag-

gerate, or timid and withdrawn? As many students as possible should have a turn at being the storyteller.

Movement, improvisation, and acting

1. Divide the class into two groups, a group of villagers and a group of spirits. Ask the students to choose a strong physical characteristic (one that can easily be identified by an onlooker) and an objective (e.g., a one-eyed spirit, wanting the sight of a graceful, energetic girl, who is going off to meet her friends).

(a) The two groups, at a given signal, advance to the middle of the rehearsal space. As they reach the centre of the room, each villager is faced by a spirit. They freeze.

(b) A signal such as a handclap starts a transformation, which takes place without speaking, and each student must assume the shape of the other person.

For example, a jack o'lantern may be standing close to a village child, a crawling thing close to an old man — each transforms into the shape of the other. When the change is complete, another signal starts the move back to the groups' original places. Each transformed couple now discusses how effective the change-over was.

2. Groups of six to eight are asked to explore a situation in which characters may leave their homes only at certain times of day. Each scene should make clear to the audience who and where the characters are; why they can leave their homes at a certain time; and whether it is possible to solve the problem. Each scene must show a moment of crisis in the situation.

3. Pairs and threes work on scenes of prophesy and fortune-telling. The scenes should show clearly the reasons why the fortune-teller is consulted, and the effect of the prophesy on the "clients".

4. Students bring pictures from books, newspapers, and magazines which show the moon in any phase. In groups (size of group depends on the demands of the illustration), whatever else is in the picture becomes the starting point for a) a tableau (of the moment when the picture was created), and b) the moment at which the tableau/picture comes to life, and dialogue is added to it.

Further texts for dramatization and improvisation

The narrative poem, "Lucy Gray", by William Wordsworth.
The ballad, "The Highwayman", by Alfred Noyes.
"Overheard on a Salt Marsh", by Harold Munro.
Act 1, Scene 1 of *Macbeth*, by William Shakespeare.

These texts offer strong characters, dialogue, and intriguing plots. There are unanswered questions in them which lend themselves to further improvisation.

Lucy Gray, for instance, just disappears on the moor. Tim the Ostler, who betrays the Highwayman, is not mentioned again. Groups may choose to improvise on the unknown fates of these characters.

Conclusion

The scripts and activities in this collection are intended to supplement whatever drama program you are now using in your classroom. I hope that you will find enough variety in them to meet the demands of children of different age groups, ethnic origins, and interests over an entire school year. But apart from adapting these plays for your own needs, you can explore many other possible sources for scripts or improvisation. There are some excellent books of plays or stories that can be adapted for the stage.

For teachers who are new to drama, a very helpful sourcebook of ideas, warm-up activities, and tips on improvisation is *Look, Listen, and Trust: A Framework for Learning through Drama*, by George Rawlins and Jillian Rich (Macmillan).

If you are looking for specifically Canadian content, there is a comprehensive guide to Canadian plays for young audiences, *Catalogue of Plays* (Playwrights Canada Press, Playwrights Union of Canada, 54 Wolseley St., 2nd floor, Toronto, Ontario M5T 1A5). Each play listed is accompanied by a brief plot summary and cast breakdown.

Talon Press in Vancouver publishes several titles in its "Theatre for the Young" series, including *The Windigo*, an Ojibway legend told by Dennis Foon; *Names and Nicknames* by James Reaney; and *A Chain of Words*, Japanese folktales told by Irene N. Watts.

New Canadian Kid by Dennis Foon (Pulp Press) is a marvelously innovative script about a young boy's experiences in his new homeland. Other superb plays include: *Drink the Mercury* in *Rare Earth*, edited by Stephen Watt and Maggie Steed (Methuen); *A Netful of Holes* in *Dead Proud*, edited by Ann Considine and Robyn Slovo (Women's Press; a collection of plays by new black women writers, suitable for junior high and older students); *Peacemaker* by David Holman in *Six T.I.E. Programmes*, selected by Christine Redington (Methuen); *The Rainbow Coloured Disco Dancer* in *Live Theatre: Four Plays for Young People*, by C.P. Taylor (Iron Press); and *The Silver Sword* by Stuart Henson, based on the novel by Ian Serailler (Heinemann; suitable for a very large cast).

Stories as well as plays may be used as the basis for improvisation or discussion. Some books that include multicultural material are: *Dancing Feathers* by Christal Kleitch and Paul Stephens (Annick), a story about a native Indian girl caught between the traditions of her people and the modern mainstream culture of North America; *How Many Miles to Babylon?* by Paula Fox (Bradbury), the story of a young black boy and the brutish teenagers he must elude; and *Tales from Gold Mountain* by Paul Yee (Groundwood), a collection of mesmerizing tales about the Chinese in America.

For more general information, Theatrebooks (25 Bloor St. W., Toronto, Ont. M4W 1A3 (416) 922-7175) has a comprehensive catalogue of books covering many kinds of films and plays, as well as theatre in education. The descriptions in this catalogue are accurate, and should be of use to any drama teacher.

Finally, let me urge you to be adventurous in searching out material for dramatization. Your own and your students' interests, experiences, needs, and readiness for particular kinds of drama should be the ultimate guide to selecting drama in your classroom.